HEALTH
AT WORK
DIRECTORY
*an employers' guide to workplace
health promotion services*

Published in 1992
Health Education Authority
Hamilton House
Mabledon Place
London WC1H 9TX

ISBN 1 85448 352 8

Typeset by Type Generation Ltd,
London

Printed by The KPC Group, London & Ashford, Kent

Disclaimer

The HEA's *Health at work directory* contains information on health services provided by non-profit making organisations and a number of professional bodies. The information has been supplied by the organisations and professional bodies. While every effort has been made to ensure the accuracy of the entries, the HEA cannot accept any liability of any kind as a result of any error or omission from the entries or which results from the use of any service included in the directory. The details in the directory are current for October 1992.

Foreword

WHY A HEALTH AT WORK DIRECTORY?

The Workplace Team of the Health Education Authority (HEA) has seen an increasing interest in workplace health promotion from all areas of employment, and is frequently asked for information outside its own operational areas. Most of the organisations which provide the required information, help or advice come from the voluntary sector, and therefore have limited or no resources to publicise their work. Many have already appeared in other directories available today, but these publications do not focus specifically on the services offered to a workplace.

As part of a statutory body with a remit 'to ensure that by year 2000 the people of England are more knowledgeable, better motivated, and more able to acquire and maintain good health', the HEA's Workplace Project decided to ask these organisations just what they could offer both an employer and an employee. A questionnaire was sent out to approximately 400 organisations and the responses received now form the main section of this publication.

Where possible, organisations have stated how they can help an employer to formulate certain health policies, as well as how they can help with an actual on-site problem or query. The information gathering has shown the depth and breadth of the non-profit making organisations which can help British industry and commerce in its workplace health promotion. We hope that you will find this directory a useful resource for your own working environment.

Jane Greenoak
Manager, Workplace Setting
Health Education Authority

Contents

Introduction

HOW TO USE THIS BOOK

Details of over 200 non-statutory organisations are included in this directory. It is hoped that the following will help you to find the information you need easily.

To enable readers to look up broad topics, organisations were asked to complete a questionnaire indicating their main and subsidiary areas of responsibility. Entries in the 'Directory of non-statutory organisations' section are grouped alphabetically by main subject area. (Subject areas are also listed, and cross-referenced, in Appendix I on p.111.) Additionally, at the end of each subject, there is a list of other organisations which put it as one of their subsidiary areas of responsibility. Page numbers for these organisations are also given.

If you want to find out if a particular organisation is listed, but are unsure which subject to look under, Appendix II (on p.113) is an alphabetical index by organisation name.

If you would like your organisation to be considered for inclusion in future editions of the *Health at work directory*, or would like to update any details in the current directory, please contact:

Workplace Office
Health Education Authority
Hamilton House
Mabledon Place
London WC1H 9TX.

All entries in the directory are free.

CONTACTING ORGANISATIONS

The organisations listed in this directory are non-profit making and therefore, in your correspondence to them, please ensure that you include a stamped self-addressed envelope (SSAE). In most cases, where it is stated that an organisation charges for products or services, these are cost-covering charges. Many organisations also have membership schemes, for which details will be provided on request. Again, these are usually at a nominal charge, which often then entitles you to regular newsletters and other information. If you do not wish to become a member, many organisations produce publications lists which are available on receipt of an SSAE.

REGIONAL UMBRELLA ORGANISATIONS

This directory is a collection of information from voluntary organisations based in England, although many of them do have nationwide support groups. If you wish to contact groups based in other parts of the country, the following organisations will be able to help.

Northern Ireland
Northern Ireland
Council for Voluntary
Action
127 Ormeau Road
Belfast BT7 1SH
Tel: (0232) 321224
Fax: (0232) 438350
Contact: Elizabeth Law

Scotland
Scottish Council for
Voluntary
Organisations
18/19 Claremont Crescent
Edinburgh EH7 4QD
Tel: (031) 556 3882
Fax: (031) 556 0279
Contact: Dot Pringle

Wales
Wales Council for
Voluntary Action
Llys Ifor
Crescent Road
Caerphilly
Mid Glamorgan CF8 1XL
Tel: (0222) 869224
Fax: (0222) 860627
Contact: Lynda Garfield

COMPLEMENTARY HEALTH CARE

The field of complementary health care is expanding rapidly and covers areas of treatment not included in the National Health Service, for example, acupuncture, herbalism, homoeopathy and osteopathy. If you have any queries on these, or any other alternative therapies, the Institute of Complementary Medicine holds the British Register of Complementary Practitioners which contains different sections for the different types of practitioner. All entries have been checked by the Institute and there is an information line available on (071) 237 5165.

For any further information please contact:
The Institute of Complementary Medicine
Suite 7, 2nd Floor
Ensign House
Admiral's Way
London E14

INDEPENDENT HEALTH CARE SERVICES

The organisations listed in this publication are mainly from the voluntary sector or are professional bodies. However, the independent sector is constantly expanding its range of services on offer to workplaces. In the United Kingdom, this sector consists of charitable and profit-making institutions who can provide services for both medical and surgical conditions as well as services for older people and people with mental or physical disabilities.

The Directory of Independent Hospitals and Health Services 1992, published by Longman in association with the Independent Healthcare Association, contains information on a variety of areas within the independent sector including details of registered private and voluntary residental care homes, nursing homes, screening clinics with their current charges, independent hospitals, and private beds in National Health Service hospitals. A copy of the 1991 edition of this publication can be seen in the Health Promotion Information Centre at the Health Education Authority (see below).

HEALTH EDUCATION AUTHORITY
WORKPLACE SERVICES

Health Education Authority
Hamilton House
Mabledon Place
London WC1H 9TX
Tel: (071) 383 3833
Fax: (071) 387 0550

The Health Education Authority (HEA) was established in 1987 as a Special Health Authority within the National Health Service serving the population of England. Although it works primarily in England it does collaborate closely with corresponding bodies in Scotland, Wales and Northern Ireland. The HEA can offer employers and employees a wide range of workplace services, with up-to-date information available from the Health Promotion Information Centre (HPIC). Except where stated below all further information can be obtained from the HPIC.

Health at Work This new HEA national initiative builds on the success of the Look After Your Heart (LAYH) Workplace Project (see below), and is designed to respond to a wider range of workplace health concerns. The Health at Work support team can help an employer to devise and co-ordinate health promotion plans and policies to meet individual company needs. Extensive back-up in the form of information and contacts is provided, either through your district or regional health authority, or specific HEA project teams, and a direct link with national health campaigns such as No Smoking Day, the Drinkwise campaign, Enjoy Healthy Eating month and Europe against Cancer. For further information please contact Jane Greenoak, HEA Workplace Manager.

Look After Your Heart in the Workplace

Look After Your Heart (LAYH) is an umbrella programme for a wide range of activities that encourage healthier lifestyles. One of these activities is the LAYH Workplace Project which encourages organisations to look after the health of their employees by introducing a wide range of activities including smoking policies, healthy eating, promoting physical activity, health checks and 'Look After Your Heart: Look After Yourself' classes run by a national network of 2,500 tutors. The Department of Employment, the CBI and the TUC are backing the initiative and many national companies have already joined. Please contact the HEA's Workplace office for further details.

The Look After Your Heart: Look After Yourself (LAYH: LAY) project aims to enable people to have a better understanding of a range of health topics such as nutrition and alcohol, and to increase their level of physical activity safely and to understand and cope with stress. The role of National Workplace Service managers is to work with national companies and government departments, providing the appropriate services to enable them to attain their health education objectives. This is achieved through a number of different activities including: staging lifestyle exhibitions, introducing lifestyle courses, providing a series of topic-based lifestyle seminars, facilitating LAYH: LAY training for staff, and incorporating elements of the programme into in-house training courses and pre-retirement programmes. In this way the project provides opportunities for individuals to obtain personally relevant information and advice, to acquire lifestyle skills and to gain a general overview of their current health status. These are designed to encourage and facilitate lifestyle changes. LAYH: LAY has proven a particularly effective and beneficial means of both introducing and developing health policies.

For further information on LAYH: LAY, please contact John Billingham, HEA Business Manager, at the HEA Business Unit, Christ Church College, Canterbury, Kent CT1 1QU; tel: (0227) 455564. If you prefer, you can go directly to your National Workplace Service Manager.

Northern, Yorkshire, North West, Mersey and Trent Regional Health Authority areas. *Contact: Linda Bond* (0709) 375091.

The four Thames Regional Health Authority areas. *Contact: Jackie Butler* (081) 393 5344.

West Midland and South Western Regional Health Authority areas. *Contact: Ann Chandler* (0527) 72625.

Oxford, Wessex and East Anglia Regional Health Authority areas. *Contact: Pamela Elder* (02357) 66683.

Cancer Education in the Workplace

The HEA, together with voluntary and statutory agencies, is committed to the Europe Against Cancer (EAC) and World Health Organization (WHO) initiatives which aim to reduce the number of deaths from cancer by 15% by the year 2000. The first phase of a workplace cancer education pilot programme was completed in June 1991. A number of organisations participated in the pilot which was based upon the EAC 10 point code and a broader collection of resources and seminars about cancer risk minimisation. The qualitative research based on this phase has served to inform development of future workplace programmes and determine guidelines and action plans for the introduction of cancer education programmes in the workplace.

For any on-site queries or problems, the Cancer Education programme can offer:

- Advice on resources about cancer and ways to minimise personal risk. The programme's resource list is a comprehensive guide to the leaflets, booklets, books and videos currently available from the HEA and other bodies;
- Information on the cancer charities and support organisations which can be contacted for advice or counselling.

These services are available to both employers and employees. If you require further information on how to formulate a cancer policy in the workplace please contact Jane Greenoak, HEA Workplace Manager.

Smoking in the Workplace

The Smoking Education programme provides support for employers and employees in the following ways.

- Advising employers wishing to formulate a smoking policy according to the HEA's current position on smoking in the workplace, and providing information on the different services available to them from LAYH Workplace Services and the other organisations such as ASH and QUIT (see directory entries in the section on smoking).
- Giving the most up-to-date information on passive smoking to those people who want to take up the issue with their employers. This includes referral to the relevant agencies who can advise on legal rights and on more general conciliatory advice e.g. going through the trade union.
- Producing information and leaflets on smoking cessation, passive smoking and telling enquirers about the smoking policies at work manual.

For further information please contact Katie Aston, HEA Smoking Programme Officer.

Alcohol in the Workplace

This project emphasises the need for responsible and appropriate drinking in the workplace. A business forum has been established as part of the project to raise alcohol awareness within companies through improved information and training, and training packs for managers and employees have recently been published. Drinkwise day, held annually in June, provides an excellent opportunity for companies to begin to raise the alcohol issue at work. Over eleven hundred companies took part in 1992, and even more will do so in 1993. For further information please contact the HEA Alcohol Programme Manager.

HIV and AIDS in the Workplace

The HIV/AIDS and Sexual Health programme regards the workplace as an important setting in which to promote better understanding and knowledge around HIV and AIDS, and has recently funded a qualitative research project on HIV and AIDS in the workplace. New materials to support workplace initiatives are currently under development. These will include posters and an information pack for employers. The programme is also supporting a number of initiatives in conjunction with other agencies. These include, in conjunction with the British Red Cross, an HIV and AIDS education project for seafarers registered with British ships, and the production of an employers guide for overseas employees. For further information please contact the HEA Workplace Office.

Nutrition in the Workplace

The nutrition programme is involved in the promotion of food policies among employers in both the public and private sector. Forthcoming publications for occupational health staff, workplace caterers and dietitians will provide practical guidelines for workplace food policy development. For further information please contact Caroline Hurren, HEA Nutrition Programme Officer.

Family and Child Health in the Workplace

Although it is not as prominent in the workplace as the other HEA programmes, all current projects of the Family and Child Health programme do consider working women. For example, parts of the *Pregnancy book* give information on work hazards, and rights and benefits. For further information please contact Karen Ford, HEA Family and Child Health Programme Officer.

The Health Promotion Information Centre

The HEA provides a wide range of resources for both specialist and general use. The Health Promotion Information Centre houses a comprehensive collection of books, reports, journals, videos, films and teaching materials from Britain and other countries; as well as covering the HEA's major programmes and settings.

The HPIC is open to health professionals, educationalists and students on courses with a health element. Library staff are available to help with research enquiries, and selected lists of references are provided on request. Resources advisers provide an advisory service on health promotion resources for use with adults and in training for health education. They evaluate training materials and arrange preview sessions of videos and training materials for health professionals.

The Health Promotion Information Centre opens 9am–5pm Monday–Friday and visitors to the HEA are welcome to take single copies of leaflets, and to make use of the centre. For any further information please contact Sue Cook, HEA Health Promotion Information Centre Manager.

NATIONAL HEALTH SERVICE WORKPLACE SERVICES

With the reformation of the NHS now firmly in progress, District and/or Regional Health Authorities should not be overlooked as possible sources of help and information. To find out what is on offer in your area, please contact your regional Look After Your Heart Workplace Officer on one of the following numbers:

Region	Officer	Telephone number
East Anglia	Chantal Bradley	(0223) 375331
Merseyside	Kate Parkes	(051) 228 1616 ext 5373
Northern	Beryl Robinson	(091) 224 6222 ext 46627
North Western	Lesley Burn	(061) 237 2744
Oxford	Sally Crowe	(0865) 226038
South Western	Miriam Glover	(0823) 333491
North West Thames	Danila Armstrong	(0438) 357512
North East Thames	HEA	(071) 383 3833
South East Thames	Mary Hart	(0892) 515152 ext 3086/7
South West Thames	Sydney Lewis	(071) 262 8011 ext 4356
Trent	Terry Bell	(0623) 21148
Wessex	Annette Rushmere	(0962) 863511
West Midlands	Carole Prichard	(021) 456 5566
Yorkshire	Lynda Koral	(0423) 500066

The Help for Health Trust

Funded by Wessex Regional Health Authority and District Health Authorities in Wessex, the trust aims to provide patients, relatives, carers, health professionals, researchers and others with ready access to relevant healthcare information. It is actively involved in promoting the concept of informed participation as an essential cornerstone of quality healthcare. Building on over ten years of experience, the comprehensive information services of the trust can give details on many of the topics covered in this publication, as well as providing a national self-help database (Helpbox), publications, training, and consultancy with services available throughout the UK on a contract basis.

For further information please contact:
Help for Health Trust
Highcroft Cottage
Romsey Road
Winchester SO22 5DH
Tel: (0962) 849100
Fax: (0962) 849079

Directory of general help and information organisations

The following organisations provide information and/or publications on health related issues in the workplace. It is hoped that the following information will help the reader to decide whether or not to approach them in preference, or in addition, to the organisations listed in the main section of this directory.

Advisory Conciliation and Arbitration Service (ACAS)
27 Wilton Street
London SW1X 7AZ
Tel: (071) 210 3000
Fax: (071) 210 3708

ACAS is a statutory body with a general duty of promoting the improvement of industrial relations and of encouraging collective bargaining. Proper concern for the health and safety of employees is an important aspect of this duty, and help is provided to employers and employee representatives in drawing up policies and procedures on health and employment related issues such as smoking and alcohol. ACAS can also provide both short and longer term counselling for employers when dealing with sickness absence related to stress, alcohol or drug issues.

A series of advisory booklets is available including one entitled *Health and employment*. ACAS does have a number of regional offices, details of which can be obtained from the information service at the above address.

British Medical Association (BMA)
BMA House
Tavistock Square
London WC1H 9JP
Tel: (071) 387 4499
Fax: (071) 383 6400

The BMA is a professional organisation established in 1832 'to promote the medical and allied sciences, and to maintain the honour and interests of the medical profession'. It represents all doctors in the UK and has a leading position in Europe. The BMA has a number of regional offices, largely providing industrial relations advice for doctors; details of these can be obtained from the headquarters at the above address.

In addition to its functions as a trade union body, working to maintain standards in the terms and conditions of service of doctors, the BMA is also a major professional organisation which formulates policy on issues of health and healthcare. In particular, there are two standing committees relating to the health in the workplace initiative. The first of these is the Occupational Health Committee which was set up to consider and report on matters that affect the health of persons at work, and the practice of medicine in industry and allied occupations. In addition, the BMA's Board of Science and Education initiates research and produces policy statements and reports on a wide range of topics concerning public health and general scientific issues. Recent reports include the *BMA guide to living with risk* (1990), which features a chapter on occupational risks, and *Alcohol and accidents* (1989), which studies the problem of alcohol related accidents at work. Two codes of practice have also been produced by the Board of Science to provide practical guidance on clinical safety and ways of maintaining standards within a healthcare setting. The BMA has also produced a number of statements and policy documents on smoking.

One of the resources of the BMA is its extensive library and information service. This is resident in BMA House and includes on-line database and search facilities, a wide range of specialist journals and books, and links with other clinical and academic organisations.

The Confederation of British Industry (CBI)

Centrepoint
103 New Oxford Street
London WC1A 1DU
Tel: (071) 379 7400
Fax: (071) 240 1578

The Confederation of British Industry, established in 1965, is Britain's leading employer's organisation. It brings together the experience of business leaders to promote the prosperity of British trade and industry. It is also the employer's representative on leading bodies such as ACAS and HSE (see relevant entries in this section).

The CBI has various committees and working groups, handling issues including health and safety; it also produces a wide range of publications. It has recently conducted a national survey on the cost of mental health to business, and held a one day conference in November 1991 with the theme of promoting mental health at work.

Department of Employment

Caxton House
Tothill Street
London SW1H 9NF

The Department of Employment produces the following guidance booklets which are aimed at stimulating employers to devise workplace policies:

- *AIDS and the workplace –
a guide for employers*
- *AIDS and work –
what employees should know*

- *Alcohol in the workplace – a guide for employers*
- *Drug misuse and the workplace – a guide for employers*

These booklets are provided free of charge from the following address:
ISCO5
The Paddock
Frizinghall
Bradford
West Yorkshire BD9 4HD

Department of Health
Richmond House
79 Whitehall
London SW1A 2NS

The Department of Health produces health information on a range of topics including HIV/AIDS, drugs misuse, women's health, guidelines for certain professions (such as acupuncture, earpiercing), travelling abroad, and the Children's Act. Most information can be obtained from:
The Health Publications Unit
Heywood Stores
Manchester Road
Heywood
Lancashire OL10 2PZ

Priced documents are available from HMSO Publications Centre, telephone orders: (071) 873 9090; general enquiries: (071) 837 0011. HMSO bookshops or accredited agents are listed in the yellow pages.

Health and Safety Executive (HSE)
Public enquiries to:

Baynards House	Broad Lane
1 Chepstow Place	Sheffield S3 7HQ
London W2 4TF	Tel: (0742) 752539
Tel: (071) 221 0870	Fax: (0742) 720006
Fax: (071) 221 9178	

The HSE is the operating arm of the Health and Safety Commission which was established by the Health and Safety at Work Act 1974. The aims of the Commission and the Executive are to protect the health, safety and welfare of employees and to safeguard others who may be exposed to risks from industrial activity. The Executive is reponsible for ensuring that the Health and Safety at Work Act is observed in the workplace. This is achieved through a network of HSE inspectors and 20 area offices throughout the country.

The HSE has several operational divisions including the Employment Medical Advisory Service (EMAS), an organisation of doctors and nurses who investigate and advice on health and work. EMAS gives free advice on request to any employee, self-employed worker, trade union representative, employer or medical practitioner on the effects of work on health, as well as providing guidance on the placement and return to work of people with health problems.

There is a wide range of HSC and HSE publications, all of which are detailed in the HSE's *Publications in series* catalogue. For this catalogue, available free of charge, and for any further information please contact the public enquiry points, HSE library and information services, at either of the above addresses. They can also give you, where applicable, the address of your area office.

The Institution of Occupational Safety and Health (IOSH)
Lawrence Corney House
222 Uppingham Road

Leicester LE5 0QG
Tel: (0533) 768424
Fax: (0533) 460423

A professional institution drawing members from those practising occupational safety and health throughout industry and commerce, IOSH aims to promote systematic and organised methods of improving occupational safety at work and to facilitate the exchange of information among members and others. It has strict membership criteria and established exams for corporate membership.

In addition to an annual conference, IOSH organises separate seminars and conferences to cater for the specialist needs of industry. It does produce publications, with emphasis on occupational safety. Members have access to a technical advice and information service.

The Institute of Personnel Management (IPM)

IPM House
Camp Road
London SW19 4UX
Tel: (081) 946 9100
Fax: (081) 947 2570

Established in 1923, IPM is the professional personnel management association covering both the UK and Ireland. It aims to influence both occupational and social environments, relevant legislation and management thinking.

IPM members have access to the IPM library and information services which contain information on health policies in the workplace as well as reading lists on occupational health services. Non-members have access to the collection for £50 per day, or part of a day. The institute has produced its own guides on smoking policies and alcohol and drug misuse at work which are available from the comunications department at the above address, to any interested party.

The Royal Institute of Public Health and Hygiene (RIPHH)

28 Portland Place
London W1N 4DE
Tel: (071) 580 2731
Fax: (071) 580 6157

The institute is a public health educational charity and as such has an interest in all of the health areas covered by this directory. It will help with queries on an ad hoc basis.

The Trades Union Congress (TUC)

Congress House
Great Russell Street
London WC1B 3LS
Tel: (071) 636 4030
Fax: (071) 636 0632

The TUC works to promote the interests of its 78 affiliated trade unions. If you have a query, please contact the social health and environment protection department at the above number, who will refer you to the appropriate local officer for your industry/profession. The TUC has produced a number of health related publications on issues such as the use of VDUs, upper limb injuries, stress and cancer. A full publications list is available on written request with a stamped addressed envelope.

Directory of non-statutory organisations by subject

ACCIDENTS/ACCIDENT PREVENTION

British Association for Immediate Care (BASICS)
7 Black Horse Lane
Ipswich
Suffolk IP1 2EF
Tel: (0473) 218407
Fax: (0473) 280585
Founded: 1977
Contact: Mr R Bailey, Chief Executive
95 other locations
No public library facilities
Workplace publications
Charge for some services/products

Concerned with extending the number of immediate care schemes in this country and the development of immediate care through training, research and communication with other services.

Royal Society for the Prevention of Accidents (ROSPA)
Cannon House
Priory Queensway
Birmingham B4 6BS
Tel: (021) 200 2461
Fax: (021) 200 1254
Founded: 1916
3 other locations
No public library facilities
Workplace publications
Charge for some services/products

Produces a wide range of publications, films, audiovisual materials and training courses on all aspects of accident prevention and health at work.

An enquiry service and library is available to members only.

Spinal Injuries Association (SIA)
Newpoint House
76 St James's Lane
London N10 3DF
Tel: (081) 444 2121
Fax: (081) 444 3761
Founded: 1976
Contact: Ms Mary-Ann Tyrrell, Administrative Director
No other locations
No public library facilities

No workplace publications
Charge for some services/products

Supports those with spinal cord injuries and helps members in their everyday lives, including achieving career objectives.

The welfare and information service helps members on an individual basis in their chosen lifestyle.

Other organisations

Association of Optometrists: **33;** British Epilepsy Association: **59;** The British Hypnotherapy Association: **76;** The Central Council of Physical Recreation: **86;** City Centre Project Ltd: **107;** The Golden Shoe Club (Safety Footwear) Ltd: **64;** Health and Safety Advice Centre: **107;** Joint Committee on Mobility for Disabled People: **50;** The Medico 9 Organisation: **62;** National Back Pain Association: **30;** The Psychotherapy Centre: **44;** Sickle Cell and Thalassaemia Information Centre: **60;** St John Ambulance: **62.**

ADDICTIONS

Community Drug Project (CDP)
30 Manor Place
London SE17 3BB
Tel: (071) 703 0559
Fax: –
Founded:1968
Contact: Any project worker
No other locations
No public library facilities
Workplace publications
Charge for some services/products

Offers counselling, advice and referral to those affected in any way by substance abuse. The service is totally confidential and training and advice can be given to employers.

The Libra Trust
93 Horseshoe Lane East
Merrow
Guildford
Surrey GU1 2TW
Tel: –
Fax: –
Founded: 1971
Contact: Mrs Fiona Rochez-Maggs
Administrator
3 other locations
No public library facilities
Workplace publications
No charge for services/products

Libra is for people affected by substance misuse, including alcohol. Support groups open to misusers, their families and interested professionals. Libra also run a 24-hour helpline and a halfway house in Sussex.

The National Council on Gambling (NCG)
Regent's Wharf
8 All Saints Road
London N1 9RE
Tel: (081) 785 9460
Fax: –
Founded: 1980
Contact: Mr E N Kent, Honorary
Secretary
2 other locations
No public library facilities
No workplace publications
Charge for some services/products

Aims to educate the general public about gambling and to help those whose participation in society is impaired by gambling.

Release
388 Old Street
London EC1V 9LT
Tel: (071) 729 9904
Fax: (071) 729 2599
Founded: 1967
Contact: Ms Jane Goodsir, Director
No other locations
No public library facilities
Workplace publications
Charge for some services/products

Advice available on legal and practical aspects of dealing with drug users affecting policy formation. Practical advice and information given on drugs and legal issues in relation to drugs and their use.

There is a 24-hour emergency telephone service available on (071) 603 8654.

Other organisations

Action Against Allergy: **26**; Bath Alcohol Advisory Centre: **24**; The British Hypnotherapy Association: **76**; Eating Disorders Association: **56**; Institute for the Study of Drug Dependence: **54**; National Association for Mental Health: **77**; The National College of Hypnosis and Psychotherapy: **43**; National Council of Psychotherapists and Hypnotherapy Register: **44**; The Psychotherapy Centre: **44**; The Samaritans: **45**; Turning Point: **55**; Women's Health: **97**.

Al-Anon Family Groups UK & Eire
61 Great Dover Street
London SE1 4YF
Tel: (071) 403 0888
Fax: –
Contact: The Public Information Secretary
No other locations
No public library facilities
Workplace publications
Charge for some services/products

Provides understanding and support for relatives and friends of problem drinkers, whether the alcoholic is still drinking or not. There is one central office which can provide details of local group meetings, and members are available to talk to groups and professionals.

Based at the same address, Alateen is for teenagers who are or who have been affected by someone else's drinking. All meetings are confidential and free of charge.

Alcohol Concern
275 Grays Inn Road
London WC1X 8QF
Tel: (071) 833 3471
Fax: (071) 278 2970
Founded: 1984
Contact: Mr Oswald O'Brien, Director of Workplace Advisory Service
No other locations
Public library facilities
Workplace publications
Charge for some services/products

Advice offered on the nature and extent of alcohol problems at work along with the necessary policies to deal with them. Training available for staff responsible for implementing policies, and links with local help agencies can be forged. Advice can be given for individual problems at work and information provided on the nearest appropriate services.

An information pack is available, plus guidance on relevant reading. Alcohol Concern's general information service and its library service are also available to enquirers and researchers on request.

Alcohol Counselling and Prevention Service
34 Electric Lane
London SW9 8JT
Tel: (071) 737 3579
Fax: –
Founded: 1977
1 other location
No public library facilities
No workplace publications
Charge for some services/products

Offers advice and consultation on the formation of alcohol policies in the workplace. Individual counselling available by arrangement. Also offers advice and training for welfare and personnel staff.

Alcoholics Anonymous (General Service Office) (GB) Ltd (AA)
PO Box 1
Stonebow House
Stonebow
York YO1 2NJ
Tel: (0904) 644026
Fax: (0904) 629091
Founded: 1935

Contact: General Secretary
Numerous other locations
No public library facilities
No workplace publications
No charge for services/products

A worldwide fellowship of men and women from all walks of life who meet to attain and maintain sobriety. The only membership requirement is a desire to stop drinking. Membership is free and there are over 2800 groups throughout the UK.

Aquarius Action Projects
6th Floor
The White House
111 New Street
Birmingham B2 4EU
Tel: (021) 632 4727
Fax: (021) 633 0539
Founded: 1977
Contact: Ms Pip Mason, Deputy Director
11 other locations
No public library facilities
Workplace publications
Charge for some services/products

Offers training and consultancy regarding the implementation of workplace policies about alcohol and drugs. Has counselling services to help employees with alcohol or drug problems and can give advice and information, group or individual counselling and residential provision.

Bath Alcohol Advisory Centre (BAAC)
10 Broad Street
Bath BA1 5LJ
Tel: (0225) 464374
Fax: –
Founded: 1983

Contact: Ms Fionnuala Coulson, Manager
4 other locations
Public library facilities
Workplace publications
No charge for services/products

As the Bath office of the Avon Council on Alcohol and Drugs, the centre offers a comprehensive range of services with expertise in developing an integrated alcohol programme which could include:

- Identification of problems and assistance for employees
- Management intervention procedures
- Prevention strategies and evaluation techniques
- Current information about alcohol and the workplace
- Educational materials and tailor-made training
- Direct access to counselling and treatment services.

Institute of Alcohol Studies (IAS)
Alliance House
12 Caxton Street
London SW1H 0QS
Tel: (071) 222 5880
Fax: (071) 799 2510
Founded: 1982
Contact: Mr A McNeill, Co-Director
1 other location
Public library facilities
Workplace publications
Charge for some services/products

Literature, advice, education and training services available to employing organisations. IAS always tries to respond helpfully to queries from employers, trade union representatives and other concerned parties in relation to an actual individual problem. No counselling services available to individual problem drinkers.

Medical Council on Alcoholism (MCA)

1 St Andrew's Place
London NW1 4LB
Tel: (071) 487 4445
Fax: –
Founded: 1967
Contact: Dr E E P Barnard, Executive Director
No other locations
Public library facilities
Workplace publications
Charge for some services/products

Primarily concerned with educating the medical professions about the effects of alcohol upon health. Handles many research enquiries.

Teetotallers Register (TT REG)

Jordans
1c Grassington Road
Eastbourne
East Sussex BN20 7BP
Tel: (0323) 638234
Fax: –
Founded: 1986
Contact: Ms Wendy Whitehead, National Compiler/Secretary
No other locations
No public library facilities
Workplace publications
No charge for services/products

Designed to encourage and support people who wish to enjoy a teetotal lifestyle. It aims to develop a creative health community network through health education and non-alcoholic social activity by promoting a totally 'stay dry' policy.

Other organisations

The British Hypnotherapy Association: **76**; Community Drug Project: **21**; Dr Jan de Winter Cancer Prevention Foundation: **36**; The Libra Trust: **21**; London Black Women Health Action Project: **60**; The National College of Hypnosis and Psychotherapy: **43**; National Council of Psychotherapists and Hypnotherapy Register: **44**; The Psychotherapy Centre: **44**; Royal Society for the Prevention of Accidents: **19**; The Samaritans: **45**; Turning Point: **55**; Women's Health: **97**.

ALLERGIES/FOOD INTOLERANCES

Action Against Allergy (AAA)
24–26 High Street
Hampton Hill
Middlesex TW11 9PA
Tel: –
Fax: (081) 943 3631
Founded: 1978
Contact: Mrs Patricia Schooling,
Executive Director
No other locations
No public library facilities
Workplace publications
No charge for services/products

Helps people with allergies solve their problems and improve their health and well being.

Food and Chemical Allergy Association
27 Ferringham Lane
Ferring
West Sussex BN12 5NP
Tel: (0903) 241178
Fax: –
Founded: 1976
Contact: Mrs E Rothera,
Chairman/Secretary
No other locations
No public library facilities
Workplace publications
No charge for services/products

Provides literature to help people trace the causes of their own ill health, covering all aspects of allergy and environmental illness. Can provide contacts with private doctors when required.

National Pollen and Hayfever Bureau (NPHB)
c/o Dept of Environmental Health & Consumer Affairs
Elm Bank House
73 Alma Road
Rotherham
South Yorks S60 2BU
Tel: (0709) 823105
Fax: (0709) 367554
Founded: 1983
Contact: Mr Bob Crosby, Senior
Executive
No other locations
No public library facilities
Workplace publications
No charge for services/products

Collates pollen counts nationally and provides advice to people with hayfever.

National Society for Research into Allergy (NSRA)
PO Box 45
Hinkley
Leicester LE10 1JY
Tel: (0455) 851546
Fax: (0455) 851546
Founded: 1980
Contact: Mrs Eunice L Rose, Founder
and Secretary
No other locations
No public library facilities
No workplace publications
Charge for some services/products

Provides information on allergies, with expertise in teaching self-help. Offers members various diets, books and magazines. Membership is open to lay and professional personnel.

Other organisations
The British Dietetic Association: **81**; The British Hypnotherapy Association: **76**; The British Nutrition

Foundation: **81**; Cystitis and Candida: **97**; The Food Commission: **81**; La Leche League (Great Britain): **102**; ME Action Campaign: **74**; National Asthma Campaign: **89**; National Council of Psychotherapists and Hypnotherapy Register: **44**; National Eczema Society: **90**; The Psychotherapy Centre: **40**; Sanity: **77**; Society for Environmental Therapy: **57**.

ARTHRITIC/RHEUMATIC DISEASES

Arthritis Care

18 Stephenson Way
London NW1 2HD
Tel: (071) 916 1500
Fax: (071) 916 1505
Founded: 1947
Contact: Mr J R Collins, Secretary
525 other locations
No public library facilities
Workplace publications
No charge for services/products

Offers information, advice and practical help to people with arthritis and those who care for them. Also campaigns for greater public awareness of needs and problems associated with arthritis. Holds regular meetings to share information, give support and organise activities. Has a special group for younger people with arthritis.

Free helpline available 1–5 pm on (0800) 289170 for anyone.

Steroid Aid Group (SAG)

The Dell
Water Lane
Sullington
Sussex RH20 3LY
Tel: (0903) 743696
Fax: –
Founded: 1979
Contact: Mrs A B Austin, Secretary
1 other location
No public library facilities
Workplace publications
No charge for services/products

Helps people to reduce their intake of steroids, or to cope with the side effects induced by steroids.

Other organisations

Action Against Allergy: **26**; Disabled Living Foundation: **50**; Food and Chemical Allergy Association: **26**; Mobility Trust: **50**; National Council of Psychotherapists and Hypnotherapy Register: **44**; National Society for Research into Allergy: **26**; The Psoriasis Association: **90**; Society for Environmental Therapy: **57**.

**Society for the Prevention of Asbestosis
and Industrial Diseases (SPAID)**
38 Drapers Road
Enfield
Middlesex EN2 8LU
Tel: (0707) 873025
Fax: –
Founded: 1978
Contact: Mrs Nancy Tate, Secretary
1 other location
No public library facilities
No workplace publications
No charge for services/products

Promotes research into the causes, prevention and remedial treatment of asbestosis and other industrial diseases and then disseminates useful results to the public. Any information gained is used to help those concerned with workplace health and safety to identify and prevent industrial diseases.

Helps people who become sick and/or disabled at work by giving help and advice in seeking compensation and/or Department of Social Security benefit claims.

Other organisations
City Centre Project Ltd: **107**; Health and Safety Advice Centre: **107**; London Hazards Centre: **107**; National Society for Clean Air and Environmental Protection: **57**; Royal Society for the Prevention of Accidents: **19**.

BACK AND OTHER PAIN

National Back Pain Association (NBPA)
31–33 Park Road
Teddington
Middlesex TW11 0AB
Tel: (081) 977 5474
Fax: (081) 943 5318
Founded: 1968
Contact: Dr M Bryn-Jones, Executive Director
40 other locations
No public library facilities
Workplace publications
Charge for some services/products

The information officer holds a wide range of information on new treatments, products and alternative medicine. The association can usually provide a sympathetic ear for back pain sufferers and helps to form and support branches.

Other organisations
Action Against Allergy: **26**; British Dental Health Foundation: **47**; Cancer Aftercare and Rehabilitation Society: **36**; Cancer Relief Macmillan Fund: **36**; City Centre Project Ltd: **107**; Disabled Living Foundation: **50**; Health and Safety Advice Centre: **107**; London Central Young Men's Christian Association: **86**; Mobility Trust: **50**; The National College of Hypnosis and Psychotherapy: **43**; National Council of Psychotherapists and Hypnotherapy Register: **44**; National Osteoporosis Society: **83**; National Society for Research into Allergy: **26**; Repetitive Strain Injury Association: **108**; Royal Society for the Prevention of Accidents: **19**; Sickle Cell and Thalassaemia Information Centre: **60**; Society for the Prevention of Asbestosis and Industrial Diseases: **29**.

BEREAVEMENT

The Compassionate Friends (TCF)
6 Denmark Street
Bristol BS1 5DQ
Tel: (0272) 292778
Fax: –
Founded: 1969
Contact: Ms Anne Pocock, National Administrator
No other locations
Public library facilities
Workplace publications
Charge for some services/products

Self-help organisation of bereaved parents offering friendship and understanding to those similarly bereaved. Publishes a quarterly newsletter and a range of leaflets dealing with the topic of bereavement in general. Postal library.

Cruse – Bereavement Care
126 Sheen Road
Richmond
Surrey TW9 1UR
Tel: (081) 940 4818
Fax: (081) 940 7638
Founded: 1959
Contact: Ms Wendy Wilson, Information Officer
180 other locations
No public library facilities
Workplace publications
Charge for some services/products

Offers counselling, advice and information to all bereaved people together with opportunities for social contact. Also runs training courses in bereavement counselling. Help given with practical problems through fact sheets and an advisory service.

Lesbian and Gay Bereavement Project
The Vaughan M Williams Centre
Colindale Hospital
London NW9 5HG
Tel: (081) 200 0511
Fax: (081) 905 9250
Founded: 1981
Contact: Mr Dudley Cave, Outreach Officer
No other locations
No public library facilities
Workplace publications
No charge for services/products

Because homosexuality is known to damage career prospects, many lesbian and gay men conceal their homosexuality at work and so do not receive any consolation on the death of a partner. The bereavement project offers a telephone support and advice service with an office staffed from 2.30–5 pm on the above telephone number and helpline information is available on (081) 455 8894.

Can also provide speakers on same-sex loss and publishes a free will form for same-sex couples, providing for the partner to be executor and sole beneficiary.

National Association of Widows (NAW)
54–57 Allison Street
Digbeth
Birmingham B5 5TH
Tel: (021) 643 8348
Fax: –
Founded: 1971
Contact: Ms Lynne Davies, Information Officer
70 other locations
No public library facilities

No workplace publications
No charge for services/products

Offers specialist advice and information to widows and to all those concerned to help widows with the problems that they face in society today. Local branches offer support, friendship and the opportunity for a fuller social life. Some local advisory services available.

Stillbirth and Neonatal Death Society (SANDS)

28 Portland Place
London W1N 4DE
Tel: (071) 436 7940
Fax: (071) 436 3715
Founded: 1978
Contact: Ms Roma Iskander, Director
200 other locations
No public library facilities
Workplace publications
Charge for some services/products

Offers support, through a network of self-help groups throughout the UK, to parents who have suffered pregnancy loss, stillbirth or neonatal death. Works to increase awareness of the needs of bereaved parents among health professionals and the general public.

Produces publications for professionals, self-help leaflets for bereaved family and friends and a newsletter.

The above telephone number is for administration and publications; helpline available on (071) 436 5881

Other organisations

Breast Care and Masectomy Association: **99**; Bridges: **49**; British Association for Counselling: **42**; The British Hypnotherapy Association: **76**; Cancer Aftercare and Rehabilitation Society: **36**; Cancer Relief Macmillan Fund: **36**; Just Ask Advisory and Counselling Service: **43**; Life: **102**; London Black Women Health Action Project: **60**; London Lighthouse: **71**; Marie Curie Cancer Care: **38**; Miscarriage Association: **100**; Multiple Births Foundation: **103**; The National College of Hypnosis and Psychotherapy: **43**; National Council of Psychotherapists and Hypnotherapy Register: **44**; National Council for One Parent Families: **104**; Post Abortion Counselling Service: **98**; The Psychotherapy Centre: **44**; The Samaritans: **45**; Sickle Cell and Thalassaemia Information Centre: **60**; Tay Sachs and Allied Diseases Association: **61**; The Topaz Line: **45**; Twins and Multiple Births Association: **104**.

BLINDNESS/VISUAL DISABILITIES

Association of Optometrists
Bridge House
233–234 Blackfriars Road
London SE1 8NW
Tel: (071) 261 9661
Fax: (071) 261 0228
Contact: Mr Ian Hunter, Secretary General
No other locations
No public library facilities
Workplace publications
Charge for some services/products

Produces a wide range of consumer leaflets available from optometrists or direct. In addition to providing general primary vision care, some members are experienced in areas such as industrial and vocational visual problems, particularly those concerning the use of VDUs, and eye protection.

International Glaucoma Association (IGA)
King's College Hospital
Denmark Hill
London SE5 9RS
Tel: (071) 737 3265
Fax: –
Founded: 1974
Contact: Mrs B M Wright, Association Secretary
No other locations
No public library facilities
Workplace publications
Charge for some services/products

Sends factual information to enquirers on all aspects of glaucoma. Questions of a general nature are answered and the association membership receives a twice-yearly newsletter and meeting invitation. Supports research into glaucoma and its treatment.

Iris Fund for Prevention of Blindness
Ground Floor
York House
199 Westminster Bridge Road
London SE1 7UT
Tel: (071) 928 7743
Fax: –
Founded: 1965
Contact: Mrs Susanna Burr, Executive Director
No other locations
Public library facilities
Workplace publications
Charge for some services/products

Primarily a fund-raising charity with no direct patient contact, but will listen to enquiries and refer to an ophthalmic consultant if appropriate. Staff are not medically qualified but can provide general information.

Optical Information Council (OIC)
57a Old Woking Road
West Byfleet
Weybridge
Surrey KT14 6LF
Tel: (0932) 353283
Fax: (0932) 345554
Founded: 1951
Contact: Mrs G Strachan-Gray, Director
No other locations
No public library facilities
Workplace publications
Charge for some services/products

Primarily responsible for the general promotion of eye care services and products available from registered optical practitioners in the United Kingdom.

Partially Sighted Society
62 Salusbury Road
London NW6 6NS
Tel: (071) 372 1551
Fax: –
Founded: 1973
Contact: Mrs Valerie Scarr, Low Vision Adviser
3 other locations
No public library facilities
Workplace publications
Charge for some services/products

Gives advice on all aspects of living with a visual loss and provides low vision assessment and training from its centres. Items for those with poor vision are available from the mail order department. Further details from the above address.

Voluntary Transcribers Group (VTG)
8 Segbourne Road
Rubery
Birmingham B45 9SX
Tel: (021) 453 4268
Fax: –
Founded: 1948
Contact: Mrs Jean Brown, Organiser
No other locations
No public library facilities
Workplace publications
No charge for services/products

Offers transcription services from print into Braille.

Other organisations
Centre for Accessible Environments: **50**; Mobility Trust: **50**; National Deaf-Blind League: **68**; Royal Society for the Prevention of Accidents: **19**; Sickle Cell and Thalassaemia Information Centre: **60**; Tay Sachs Screening Group(Manchester): **61**.

British Association of Cancer United Patients (BACUP)
3 Bath Place
Rivington Street
London EC2A 3JR
Tel: (071) 696 9003
Fax: (071) 696 9002
Founded: 1985
Contact: Ms Nicola Hill, Press Officer
1 other location
No public library facilities
Workplace publications
Charge for some services/products

Provides a free telephone and counselling service giving advice and information on all aspects of cancer.

Freefone numbers: (071) 613 2121 (London callers only); (0800) 181199 (outside London).

Provides a range of 41 booklets on site-specific cancers and aspects of living with cancer.

Personal counselling available at the London offices. Call (071) 696 9000 for an appointment.

British Colostomy Association (BCA)
15 Station Road
Reading
Berks RG1 1LG
Tel: (0734) 391537
Fax: (0734) 569095
Founded: 1963
Contact: Mrs Cathy Richards, Director of Services
22 other locations
No public library facilities
Workplace publications
No charge for services/products

Promotes the welfare and rehabilitation of those who will undergo or have undergone a colostomy. The 200 volunteers have all overcome the psychological, emotional and practical difficulties of living with a colostomy and are available on request to visit people in hospital or at home. There are also 22 area organisers who make visits and provide a help-line service from their homes. Head office offers a letter and telephone help service and publishes patient information on dealing with practical and emotional problems, but the association cannot deal with medical matters.

Cancerlink
17 Britannia Street
London WC1Z 9JN
Tel: (071) 833 2451
Fax: (071) 833 4963
Founded: 1982
Contact: Mr Mike Beiber, Director
1 other location
No public library facilities
Workplace publications
Charge for some services/products

Provides emotional support and information on all aspects of cancer in response to telephone and letter enquiries from people with cancer, their families, friends, and professionals working with them.

Acts as a resource for over 350 cancer support and self-help groups throughout Britain and helps to set up new groups. Produces a wide range of publications on the emotional and practical issues surrounding cancer.

Cancer Aftercare and Rehabilitation Society (CARE)
21 Zetland Road
Redland
Bristol BS6 7AH
Tel: (0272) 427419
Fax: –
Founded: 1971
Contact: Mrs Anne Howard, Administrator
36 other locations
No public library facilities
Workplace publications
Charge for some services/products

Offers emotional support and practical help to people with cancer, their relatives and friends. All services are free.

Cancer Relief Macmillan Fund (CRMF)
15/19 Britten Street
London SW3 3TZ
Tel: (071) 351 7811
Fax: (071) 376 8098
Founded: 1911
Contact: Ms Loretta F Tinckham, Macmillan Services Development Manager
1 other location
No public library facilities
Workplace publications
No charge for services/products

Provides professional advice and support through a network of Macmillan nursing services, nurse and medical education and support posts in cancer care and palliative care established with initial grants from CRMF. Supports people with cancer and their families, gives information on services available and provides grants.

Cancer Winners Self Help Group
Omega House
New Street
Margate
Kent CT9 1EG
Tel: (0843) 297360
Fax: –
Founded: 1983
Contact: Secretary
No other locations
No public library facilities
No workplace publications
No charge for services/products

Offers help to cancer sufferers, their families and friends with either practical or emotional problems. Holds a small library of books and tapes which members can borrow.

Dr Jan de Winter Cancer Prevention Foundation
6 New Road
Brighton
Sussex BN1 1UF
Tel: (0273) 727213
Fax: (0273) 748915
Founded: 1982
Contact: Dr Jan de Winter, Director
No other locations
No public library facilities
No workplace publications
Charge for some services/products

Offers free advice and information on diet, exercise and avoidance of stress. Nutritional and slimming advice amplified by cookery demonstrations and lunchtime restaurant facilities. Also runs weekly meditation classes and can give psychological consultations and psychotherapy.

Early detection facilities are available on demand including blood cholesterol estimation, mammography and ultrasound screening for abnormalities in ovary, testis, aorta, kidney, liver and gallbladder.

Elimination of Leukaemia Fund (ELF)
17 Venetian Road
London SE5 9RR
Tel: (071) 737 4141
Fax: –
Founded: 1977
Contact: Mr Martyn Hall, Director
No other locations
No public library facilities
No workplace publications
No charge for services/products

Offers advice on all aspects of leukaemia and related blood disorders such as lymphomas. Will advise sufferers, their families and friends. Raises funds to improve facilities for the care and treatment of people with leukaemia.

Hodgkin's Disease Association (HDA)
PO Box 275
Haddenham
Aylesbury
Bucks HP17 8JJ
Tel: (0844) 291500
Fax: –
Founded: 1986
Contact: Mr Colin Mitchell, Co-ordinator
No other locations
No public library facilities
Workplace publications
No charge for services/products

Supplies emotional support and information to people with Hodgkin's disease and non-Hodgkin's lymphoma, their families, carers and friends.

Leukaemia Care Society
14 Kingfisher Court
Venny Bridge
Pinhoe
Exeter
Devon EX4 8JN
Tel: (0392) 64848
Fax: –
Founded: 1967
Contact: Mr F W Connett, Administrator
No other locations
No public library facilities
Workplace publications
No charge for services/products

Offers limited financial assistance, caravan holidays, support and friendship to people with leukaemia and allied blood disorders and their families via volunteers throughout the country.

Leukaemia Research Fund
43 Great Ormond Street
London WC1N 3JJ
Tel: (071) 405 0101
Fax: (071) 242 1488
Founded: 1960
Contact: Mr G R May, Administrator
240 other locations
No public library facilities
Workplace publications
No charge for services/products

Offers an information service on the various forms of leukaemia and associated blood disorders. A series of patient information booklets is available free of charge. Please ring for a list of titles.

Marie Curie Cancer Care
28 Belgrave Square
London SW1X 8QG
Tel: (071) 235 3325
Fax: (071) 823 2380
Founded: 1948
Contact: Ms Claire Batchelor,
Marketing Services Manager
13 other locations
No public library facilities
Workplace publications
No charge for services/products

Gives assistance and support to people
with cancer and their families through
residential centres and community
nursing.

The National Association of
Laryngectomee Clubs (NALC)
Ground Floor
6 Rickett Street
London SW6 1RU
Tel: (071) 381 9993
Fax: –
Founded: 1976
Contact: Miss L Abrams, General
Secretary
80 other locations
No public library facilities
Workplace publications
Charge for some services/products

Promotes the welfare and rehabilitation of those who have undergone a
laryngectomy operation. Can also
offer appropriate services for those
professionals in the medical field dealing with this group.

Regional Oncology Support Service (ROSS)
Social Oncology Department
North Western RHA
Gateway House
Piccadilly South

Manchester M60 7LP
Tel: (061) 237 2153
Fax: (061) 237 2049
Founded: 1986
Contact: Ms Trish Jones, Regional
Smoking/Cancer Programme Health
Promotion
No other locations
No public library facilities
Workplace publications
Charge for some services/products

Concerned primarily with the control
of cancer within the north western
region but provides some national services. The workplace is important as a
point of access to people of working
age for whom the cancer public education programme is appropriate, and to
inform and encourage compliance
with safety measures concerning
industrial carcinogens.

ROSS provides advice on request
but more involved problems may
justify a cost-covering charge. Con-
sultancies for industry/programme
specific tasks and training are
accepted.

Save Our Sons (SOS)
Tides Reach
1 Kite Hill
Wootton Bridge
Isle of Wight PO33 4LA
Tel: (0983) 882876
Fax: –
Founded: 1985
Contact: Ms Shirley Wilcox, Founder
No other locations
No public library facilities
Workplace publications
No charge for services/products

Provides information and emotional
support for men and boys with testic-

ular cancer. Advice given by a qualified nurse who will listen and offer help where possible.

Tenovus Cancer Information Centre
142 Whitchurch Road
Cardiff CF4 3NA
Tel: (0222) 619846
Fax: (0222) 619288
Founded: 1969
Contact: Ms Carolyn Spanswick,
Oncology Nurse Specialist
No other locations
Public library facilities
Workplace publications
No charge for services/products

Offers an information service on all aspects of cancer and provides practical and emotional support for cancer patients and their families. Activities include mobile clinics, cervical screening and general health checks by female doctors. A telephone helpline is available on (0222) 691998.

A support group meets monthly in Cardiff. The information service provides up-to-date publications on all aspects of cancer.

Women's Nationwide Cancer Control Campaign (WNCCC)
Suna House
128–130 Curtain Road
London EC2A 3AR
Tel: (071) 729 4688
Fax: (071) 613 0771
Founded: 1965
Contact: Ms Judy Harding,
Administrator
No other locations
Public library facilities
Workplace publications
Charge for some services/products

Supports and encourages the provision of facilities for the early diagnosis of cancer. Engages in public education about cancer prevention and provides an information service for women seeking assistance.

Other organisations
Breast Care and Masectomy Association: **99**; The British Dietetic Association: **81**; Brook Advisory Centres: **40**; Family Planning Association: **40**; Health and Safety Advice Centre: **107**; Just Ask Advisory and Counselling Services: **43**; Marie Stopes International: **40**; The National College of Hypnosis and Psychotherapy: **43**; National Council of Psychotherapists and Hypnotherapy Register: **44**; Society for the Prevention of Asbestosis and Industrial Diseases: **29**; Women's Health: **97**; Women's Health Concern Ltd: **99**.

CONTRACEPTION

Brook Advisory Centres
153a East Street
London SE17 2SD
Tel: (071) 708 1234
Fax: (071) 708 1390
Founded: 1964
Contact: Dr Margaret Jones, General Secretary
8 other locations
No public library facilities
Workplace publications
Charge for some services/products

Will discuss issues relating to counselling, confidentiality and personal relationships with employers with a view to forming policies. Can offer employers a contraceptive service for their staff to include counselling, advice and teaching on methods of contraception, help with relationship problems and advice concerning HIV transmission and infection.

Family Planning Association (FPA)
27–35 Mortimer Street
London W1N 7RJ
Tel: (071) 636 7866
Fax: (071) 436 3288
Founded: 1930
Contact: Ms Doreen Massey, Director
4 other locations
Public library facilities
Workplace publications
Charge for some services/products

The FPA's education and training department offers staff training, needs analysis and custom-made training and consultancy on the development of policies in relation to sexual health.

It also offers a training course for personnel staff on HIV policy and the workplace.

The FPA provides a national information and enquiry service for consumers and professionals on all aspects of family planning, sexual and reproductive health. The library is for reference only.

Marie Stopes International
108 Whitfield Street
London W1P 6BE
Tel: (071) 388 0662/2585
Fax: (071) 383 7196
Founded: 1925
Contact: Ms Julie Douglas, Client Services Manager
2 other locations
No public library facilities
Workplace publications
Charge for some services/products

Initially a provider of contraceptive advice, Marie Stopes clinics now offer comprehensive health screening to men and women at an affordable cost and with the time to talk. The majority of practitioners are women and their approach is very informal with patients able to see their own clinic notes.

Other services include pregnancy testing, counselling and abortion referral, menopause clinic, premenstrual syndrome clinic, sterilisation, and company health screening.

An advice line is available for medical queries on (071) 388 0662/8090 (ask for advice sister).

The Medical Education Trust
79 St Mary's Road
Huyton
Liverpool L36 5SR
Tel: (051) 489 5996
Fax: –
Founded: 1979
Contact: Dr Peggy Norris, Honorary Secretary
No other locations
No public library facilities
Workplace publications
Charge for some services/products

Leaflets available on contraception, health hazards, abortion, hazards to health and informed consent, pre-natal screening, *What you need to know* series, and infertility.

National Association of Natural Family Planning Teachers (NANFPT)
24 Selly Wick Drive
Selly Park
Birmingham B29 7JH
Tel: (021) 472 3806
Fax: (021) 472 0061
Founded: 1984
Contact: Dr Patricia James, Secretary
1 other location
No public library facilities
Workplace publications
Charge for some services/products

Provides education in fertility awareness, and new technological devices to detect fertility. Researches into fertility; organises courses and conferences for various interested groups, and provides clinical services for patients.

Other organisations
Cystitis and Candida: **97**; The Herpes Association: **90**; La Leche League (Great Britain): **102**; National Council for One Parent Families: **104**; Post Abortion Counselling Service: **98**; Sickle Cell and Thalassaemia Information Centre: **60**; Women's Health: **97**; Women's Health Information and Support Centre: **97**.

COUNSELLING/PSYCHOTHERAPY

British Association for Counselling (BAC)
1 Regent Place
Rugby
Warwickshire CV21 2PJ
Tel: (0788) 578328
Fax: (0788) 562189
Founded: 1977
Contact: Information and
Publications Office
No other locations
No public library facilities
Workplace publications
Charge for some services/products

Offers publications and advice on the benefits of counselling in the workplace with information on how to set up a counselling service, or providing counselling for employees without an in-house service.

Can provide people requiring counselling with a list of organisations and local practitioners.

British Association of Psychotherapists
37 Mapesbury Road
London NW2 4HJ
Tel: (081) 452 9823
Fax: (081) 452 5182
Founded: 1951
Contact: Mrs J Lawrence, Administrator
No other locations
No public library facilities
Workplace publications
Charge for some services/products

Those seeking help can telephone for the name and number of an experienced therapist with whom they can discuss whether psychotherapy would be an appropriate form of help and treatment. If treatment is recommended a referral to another qualified psychotherapist is arranged.

Counselling, Help and Advice Together (CHAT)
Royal College of Nursing
20 Cavendish Square
London W1M 0AB
Tel: (071) 629 3870
Fax: –
Founded: 1980
Contact: Mr Colin Somerville, Senior
Counsellor
No other locations
No public library facilities
Workplace publications
No charge for services/products

A personal, confidential counselling service for all nurses (whether or not they are a member of the Royal College of Nursing). The counsellors and advisors can offer counselling, help and information on a very wide range of subjects.

Crisis Counselling for Alleged Shoplifters (CCAS)
PO Box 147
Stanmore
Middlesex HA7 4YT
Tel: (081) 202 5787
Fax: –
Founded: 1981
Contact: Ms Regina Dollar, Co-chair
No other locations
No public library facilities
Workplace publications
No charge for services/products

Provides counselling and other general advice to those accused of alleged shoplifting offences. The service is given on the telephone and is confidential. Other telephone numbers are: (071) 222 3685 and, 7–10 pm, (081) 958 8859.

Identity Counselling Service
St Marylebone Healing and
Counselling Centre
17 Marylebone Road
London NW1 5LT
Tel: (071) 487 3797
Fax: –
Founded: 1978
Contact: Joint Co-ordinator
No other locations
No public library facilities
No workplace publications
Charge for some services/products

Offers counselling for people with sexual, personal, relationship and identity difficulties. Contact is via telephone or letter, and an assessment interview is held with a trained counsellor. A referral to an identity counsellor will be made for ongoing counselling.

Institute of Psychosexual Medicine
11 Chandos Street
Cavendish Square
London W1M 9DE
Tel: (071) 580 0631
Fax: –
Founded: 1974
Contact: Dr Dorothy S Howell,
Honorary Secretary
1 other location
No public library facilities
No workplace publications
Charge for some services/products

Promotes psychosexual medicine through seminar training and research. Full particulars of clinic locations and times throughout the UK are available from the above office. Any counselling/therapy offered under the NHS is free. For private consultations or therapy the fees chargeable are

agreed between the patient and individual doctors.

Just Ask Advisory and Counselling Service
46 Bishopsgate
London EC2
Tel: (071) 628 3380
Fax: –
Founded: 1979
Contact: Ms Davina M Lilley,
Director
No other locations
No public library facilities
No workplace publications
No charge for services/products

An advisory and counselling service for young people which offers specific help to the low waged or unemployed. Telephone for an appointment.

The National College of Hypnosis and Psychotherapy (NCHP)
12 Cross Street
Nelson
Lancashire BB9 7EN
Tel: (0282) 699378
Fax: (0282) 698633
Founded: 1977
Contact: Mr P J D Savage, Principal
3 other locations
No public library facilities
Workplace publications
Charge for some services/products

Can produce specifically tailored training courses in hypnotherapy, psychotherapy, and counselling to counter adverse psychological, emotional, stress and other health related phenomena in any given environment. Training can be at one of the college's centres or on employer's premises. Problems and queries are referred to the associate body, the

National Register of Hypnotherapists and Psychotherapists at the same address.

National Council of Psychotherapists and Hypnotherapy Register
46 Oxhey Road
Oxhey
Watford WD1 4QQ
Tel: (0923) 227772
Fax: –
Founded: 1971
Contact: Mr William Broom, Secretary/Treasurer
No other locations
No public library facilities
Workplace publications
Charge for some services/products

Confidential consultations and therapeutic strategies for help in overcoming emotional, behavioural, habitual and relationship problems are offered, as well as assistance for promoting more positive attitudes towards reducing the effects of physical illness. Queries regarding practitioner availability and/or suitability are dealt with by post and telephone.

Parentline
Rayfa House
57 Hart Road
Thundersley
Essex SS7 3PD
Tel: (0268) 757077
Fax: (0268) 757039
Founded: 1978
Contact: Mrs Carole Baisden, Director
24 other locations
No public library facilities
Workplace publications
No charge for services/products

Offers a confidential and anonymous telephone helpline service for parents. All volunteers are parents themselves and their main role is to listen and offer support. Where appropriate, they will also help parents to obtain professional help.

Portia Trust
Workspace
Maryport
Cumbria CA15 8NF
Tel: (0900) 812114
Fax: (0900) 812114
Founded: 1974
Contact: Mr Ken Norman, Organiser
No other locations
No public library facilities
Workplace publications
Charge for some services/products

Makes known the danger of shopping in a supermarket when in stress, confusion or haste, or in any situation in which part of the mind is involved with personal problems. Can be contacted out of office hours on (0900) 812379.

The Psychotherapy Centre
1 Wythburn Place
Marble Arch
London W1H 5WL
Tel: (071) 723 6173
Fax: –
Founded: 1960
Contact: Secretary
No other locations
No public library facilities
Workplace publications
Charge for some services/products

Can help organisations and individuals to formulate policies to avoid or identify or tackle emotional problems, including relationship problems, leadership difficulties, speech and communication problems and faulty behaviour patterns.

All practitioners have had at least four years of relevant training and take on patients for individual therapy.

Relate
Herbert Gray College
Little Church Street
Rugby CV21 3AP
Tel: (0788) 573241
Fax: (0788) 538007
Founded: 1938
Contact: Mrs Marj Thoburn, Head of Project Development
180 other locations
No public library facilities
Workplace publications
No charge for services/products

Relate offers counselling and therapy to individuals and couples experiencing relationship and sexual difficulties. Contributions are requested to cover costs.

The Samaritans
10 The Grove
Slough
Berks SL1 1QP
Tel: (0753) 532713
Fax: (0753) 524332
Founded: 1953
Contact: Ms Christine Reeves, Director of Administration and Planning
196 other locations
No public library facilities
Workplace publications
Charge for some services/products

It is widely recognised that personal problems cause lost time at work. By offering a confidential listening service 24-hours a day, 365 days a year, The Samaritans can help those who are in despair and who may be feeling suicidal.

The Topaz Line
BM/Topaz
London WC1N 3XX
Tel: –
Fax: –
Founded: 1988
Contact: Ms Sarah Bailey, Co-ordinator
No other locations
No public library facilities
No workplace publications
No charge for services/products

Free and friendly postal counselling for problems people find hard to discuss, which may not be catered for by more conventional approaches, or be within financial or other reach.

People can keep their personal identity private if they wish; personal beliefs are taken into account and practical strategies offered for coping.

Westminster Pastoral Foundation
(WPF Counselling)
23 Kensington Square
London W8 5HN
Tel: (071) 937 6956
Fax: (071) 937 1767
Founded: 1969
Contact: Dr Tim Woolmer, Director
51 other locations
No public library facilities
Workplace publications
Charge for some services/products

A professional service of counselling/psychotherapy for people with emotional, psychological, family or marital problems. Special services are provided for people suffering from serious physical illness and, where appropriate, their families. Self-referral by telephone or letter.

Training courses in counselling skills available to managers, personnel officers, occupational health personnel.

Other organisations

Action and Research for Multiple Sclerosis: **80**; Action on Phobias: **85**; Alcohol Counselling and Prevention Service: **23**; Anorexia Anonymous: **56**; Aquarius Action Projects: **24**; Association for Post Natal Illness: **101**; Bath Alcohol Advisory Centre: **24**; Brent Sickle Cell and Thalassaemia Centre: **60**; Bridges: **49**; British Association of Cancer United Patients: **35**; The British Hypnotherapy Association: **76**; Brook Advisory Centres: **40**; Cancer Aftercare and Rehabilitation Society: **36**; Cancer Relief Macmillan Fund: **36**; Cruse – Bereavement Care: **31**; Cystitis and Candida: **97**; Dr Jan de Winter Cancer Prevention Foundation: **36**; Exploring Parenthood: **102**; Helen Arkell Dyslexia Centre: **93**; The Herpes Association: **90**; Hungerford Drug Project: **54**; International Audiology Society: **67**; Life: **102**; London Black Women Health Action Project: **60**; London Central Young Men's Christian Association: **86**; London Lighthouse: **71**; Marie Stopes International: **40**; Miscarriage Association: **100**; National Association for Mental Health: **77**; The National Association of Laryngectomee Clubs: **38**; National Association of Widows: **31**; National Childbirth Trust: **103**; National Society for Research into Allergy: **26**; Partially Sighted Society: **34**; Positively Women: **71**; Post Abortion Counselling Service: **98**; Premenstrual Society: **106**; The Psoriasis Association: **90**; Regional Oncology Support Service: **38**; Release: **21**; Sickle Cell and Thalassaemia Information Centre: **60**; Spinal Injuries Association: **19**; St Bartholomew's Worried Well Centre: **72**; Tenovus Cancer Information Centre: **39**; Turning Point: **55**; United Kingdom Thalassaemia Society: **69**; Women's Health: **97**; Women's Health Concern Ltd: **99**; Women's Nationwide Cancer Control Campaign: **39**; 493 Project: **55**.

DENTAL HEALTH

British Dental Health Foundation

Eastlands Court
St Peter's Road
Rugby
Warwickshire CV21 3QP
Tel: (0788) 546365
Fax: (0788) 546365
Founded: 1971
*Contact: Mr Eric Ingham, Chief
Executive*
No other locations
No public library facilities
Workplace publications
Charge for some services/products

Promotes the benefits of dental health
to the public and offers independent
advice on all aspects of dental health or
dental-related problems.

British Fluoridation Society (BFS)

4th Floor
Dental School
University of Liverpool
PO Box 147
Liverpool L69 3BX
Tel: (051) 706 5216
Fax: (051) 706 5845
Founded: 1969
*Contact: Mrs Sheila Jones,
Information Officer*
1 other location
No public library facilities
No workplace publications
No charge for services/products

Can advise on all aspects of water
fluoridation including government/
health service policy, benefits, medical
aspects and ethical issues.

Other organisations

Action Against Allergy: **26**; Sickle
Cell and Thalassaemia Information
Centre: **60**.

DIABETES

British Diabetic Association (BDA)
10 Queen Anne Street
London W1M 0BD
Tel: (071) 323 1531
Fax: (071) 637 3644
Founded: 1934
Contact: Mrs S Redmond, Head of
Diabetes Care Department
No other locations
No public library facilities
Workplace publications
No charge for services/products

Can give advice on employing people
with diabetes as well as on all aspects
of living with diabetes.

Diabetes Foundation
177a Tennison Road
London SE25 5NF
Tel: (081) 656 5467
Fax: –
Founded: 1982
Contact: Mr Arthur Bennett,
Co-ordinator
No other locations
No public library facilities
Workplace publications
Charge for some services/products

Raises research funds and represents
the interests of all diabetics. Helpline
especially useful to newly diagnosed
diabetics and parents of diabetic
children.

Other organisations
The British Dietetic Association: **81.**

DISABILITIES

Association of Disabled Professionals (ADP)
170 Benton Hill
Horbury
West Yorkshire WF4 5HW
Tel: (0924) 270335
Fax: (0924) 276498
Contact: Miss S J Maynard, Honorary Secretary
No other locations
No public library facilities
No workplace publications
Charge for some services/products

Members are drawn from almost all professions and the majority are themselves people with disabilities. They act as advisers to people with disabilities wishing to join a profession or finding themselves, as professionals, newly disabled. Also acts as a pressure group and publishes a quarterly house bulletin for members.

Bridges
Administrative Office
New Street
Ross-on-Wye
Herefordshire HR9 7DA
Tel: (0989) 750297
Fax: (0989) 768337
Founded: 1973
Contact: Ms Shirley Eveleigh, Administrator
No other locations
No public library facilities
Workplace publications
Charge for some services/products

Formerly The Association of Professions for Mentally Handicapped People, Bridges promotes the general welfare of people with learning disabilities and their families by:

- Encouraging high standards of care and development
- Facilitating co-operation and the sharing of knowledge among professional workers
- Offering a unified professional view on the strategies of learning disability
- Educating the public to accept, understand and respect people with learning disabilities.

Has published a number of relevant reports and papers.

British Council of Organisations of Disabled People (BCODP)
De Bradelei House
Chapel Street
Belper
Derbyshire DE56 1AR
Tel: (0773) 828182
Fax: (0773) 829672
Founded: 1981
Contact: Ms Anne Rae, Development Officer
No other locations
No public library facilities
No workplace publications
No charge for services/products

Consists of 70 member organisations who represent 100,000 people with disabilities. The council represents people with disabilities on disability issues through consultative bodies and local authorities. It seeks and co-ordinates the views of members through conferences and seminars and can provide speakers on disability related issues to any organisation, subject to approval by the management committee. Minicom: (0773) 828195.

Centre for Accessible Environments
35 Great Smith Street
London SW1P 3BJ
Tel: (071) 222 7980
Fax: –
Founded: (1969)
Contact: Ms Tessa Palfreyman,
Information Officer
No other locations
Public library facilities
Workplace publications
Charge for some services/products

The centre is an information and training resource offering technical assistance with the practicalities of designing buildings that meet the needs of employees and visitors with disabilities. It publishes design guidance and a journal, *Access by design*.

Disabled Living Foundation (DLF)
380 Harrow Road
London W9 2HU
Tel: (071) 289 6111
Fax: (071) 266 2922
Founded: 1971
Contact: Information Officer
No other locations
No public library facilities
Workplace publications
Charge for some services/products

Gives practical, up-to-date, unbiased information and advice on all aspects of disability, especially equipment and problems of daily living. Displays and demonstrates equipment, runs training courses and study days. Produces a wide range of publications, advice notes and resource papers as well as teaching packs.

A telephone advice line is open weekdays 10.00–4.30; visitors welcome by appointment; reference library available by appointment.

Joint Committee on Mobility for Disabled People (JCMD)
Woodcliff House
51a Cliff Road
Weston Super Mare
Avon BS22 9SE
Tel: (0934) 642313
Fax: –
Founded: 1961
Contact: Mr Tim Shapley, Secretary
No other locations
No public library facilities
Workplace publications
No charge for services/products

Works primarily in the area of policy formation, seeking to establish principles and effective strategies through which the indoor and outdoor mobility and access needs of people with disabilities can be met. Seeks legislative changes where needed and encourages the provision of access information by transport operators and other relevant authorities.

Mobility Trust
4 Hughes Mews
143a Chatham Road
London SW11 6HJ
Tel: (071) 924 3597
Fax: (071) 924 3938
Founded: 1977
Contact: Mr Peter Mahon, Director
12 other locations
Public library facilities
No workplace publications
No charge for services/products

The trust works to help people with mental and physical disabilities become more mobile in both mind and body in the community. It can assist by loaning in perpetuity, or until such time as the recipient has no further use for it, a piece of equipment, aid or technological device. Sometimes gives interest free loans for motor vehicle adaptations.

A series of one-day seminars on the problems of living with disability, and drama-related workshops are also offered.

The National Association of Disablement Information and Advice Lines (DIAL UK)

Park Lodge
St Catherine's Hospital
Tickhill Road
Balby
Doncaster DN4 8QN
Tel: (0302) 310123
Fax: (0302) 310404
Founded: 1981
Contact: Mr Norman Witter, Director
120 other locations
No public library facilities
Workplace publications
Charge for some services/products

Provides a free, impartial and confidential service of information and advice on all aspects of disablement to people with disabilities, carers and professional service providers. The information is provided by people with direct experience of disability, through a national network of local groups.

Network for the Handicapped Ltd (NETWORK)

16 Princeton Street
London WC1R 4BB
Tel: (071) 831 8031
Fax: (071) 831 5582

Founded: 1975
Contact: Mrs Helen Berent, Secretary/ Co-ordinator
No other locations
No public library facilities
No workplace publications
No charge for services/products

Provides legal advice and assistance to people with disabilities (both physical and mental) and to their families. It covers education, consumer rights, housing, housing benefit, care and wardship proceedings, and all matters relating to income support and the social security system, complaints to the ombudsman and appeals to the social security commissioners or the high court of justice. Can advise on wills and trusts and assist in small probate matters. Please telephone to make an appointment.

Opportunities for People with Disabilities

1 Bank Buildings
Princes Street
London EC2R 8EU
Tel: (071) 726 4961
Fax: –
Founded: 1980
Contact: Ms Alison Smithson, Director General
9 other locations
No public library facilities
No workplace publications
No charge for services/products

Regional offices act as employment services for people with disabilities of all kinds, and work with local employers and other networks to help people with disabilities to find and keep productive work. The charity is also heavily involved as a sponsor in the sheltered placement scheme and runs job clubs for people with disabilities in Birmingham and London.

Outset – Action on Disability
Drake House
18 Creekside
London SE8 3DZ
Tel: (081) 692 7141
Fax: (081) 469 2532
Contact: Ms Fiona Dawe, Director, External Relations
9 other locations
No public library facilities
Workplace publications
Charge for some services/products

Promotes training and employment for people with disabilities, focussing on information technology. Outset Office Services provides sheltered employment to disabled people in office bureaux and a mailing house. Disability awareness training, consultancy and research services on all aspects of disability in the workforce for employers from all sectors are also provided.

Queen Elizabeth's Foundation for the Disabled (QEFD)
Leatherhead Court
Woodlands Road
Leatherhead
Surrey KT22 0BN
Tel: (0372) 842204
Fax: (0372) 844072
Founded: 1934
Contact: Mr Malcolm Clark, Director
6 other locations
No public library facilities
No workplace publications
Charge for some services/products

Offers a variety of services to people with disabilities including a vocational training college to help those back to employment who can no longer follow their former career. Gives advice on any aspect of outdoor mobility, general information and on micro-electronic communication equipment.

Royal Association for Disability and Rehabilitation (RADAR)
25 Mortimer Street
London W1N 8AB
Tel: (071) 637 5400
Fax: (071) 637 1827
Founded: 1977
Contact: Employment Policy Officer
No other locations
No public library facilities
Workplace publications
Charge for some services/products

Produces a fact sheet, *Guidelines for policies on the employment of disabled people*. RADAR's employment officer works on all areas concerning the employment of people with disabilities for both employee and employer.

Skill: National Bureau for Students with Disabilities
336 Brixton Road
London SW9 7AA
Tel: (071) 274 0565
Fax: (071) 274 7840
Founded: 1975
Contact: Ms Emma Delap, Information Officer
No other locations
No public library facilities
Workplace publications
Charge for some services/products

Aims to develop opportunities in further and higher education for people with disabilities and learning difficulties. Provides information to individuals on request. Membership open to any interested organisation.

Other organisations
Action and Research for Multiple Sclerosis: **80**; British Epilepsy Association: **59**; The British Hypnotherapy Association: **76**; Family Planning Association: **40**; Helen Arkell Dyslexia Centre: **93**; London Black Women Health Action Project: **60**; ME Action Campaign: **74**; Multiple Births Foundation: **103**; The Psoriasis Association: **90**; Repetitive Strain Injury Association: **108**; Sickle Cell and Thalassaemia Information Centre: **60**; Society for the Prevention of Asbestosis and Industrial Diseases: **29**; Spinal Injuries Association: **19**; Twins and Multiple Births Association: **104**; Women's Health: **97**.

DRUGS

Alcohol and Drug Addiction Prevention and Treatment Ltd (ADAPT)
Barley Wood Clinic
Long Lane
Wrington
Avon BS18 7SA
Tel: (0934) 863355
Fax: (0934) 863272
Founded: 1990
Contact: Ms Jill Lewis, Head of Nursing
No other locations
No public library facilities
No workplace publications
Charge for some services/products

A clinic for the treatment of alcohol and drug problems. In addition to its various recovery programmes, it can also offer help to companies who wish to develop a policy on alcohol and drug addiction by offering information to personnel staff and managers, assistance with assessment and advice on how to intervene.

When an employee is referred for residential treatment the clinic staff will work closely with the employer in order to facilitate discharge and a successful return to work.

Families Anonymous (FA)
Room 8
650 Holloway Road
London N19 3NU
Tel: (071) 281 8889
Fax: –
Founded: 1980
Contact: Office
36 other locations
No public library facilities
Workplace publications
Charge for some services/products

A fellowship of self-help groups for those concerned about drug abuse, or related behavioural problems of a relative or friend. It is based on the 'twelve steps' of Alcoholics Anonymous. The programme is anonymous and no fees are required. Newcomers are welcome without prior arrangement. Charges are made for booklets only.

Hungerford Drug Project
32a Wardour Street
Soho
London W1V 3HJ
Tel: (071) 437 3523
Fax: (071) 287 1274
Founded: 1970
Contact: Any project worker
40 other locations
No public library facilities
No workplace publications
No charge for services/products

Offers advice, information, counselling and referral where appropriate to drug users and those whose lives are affected by drug users. The latter can also receive training in dealing with drug users.

The Hungerford Drug Project is part of Turning Point (see p. 57). Turning Point will deal with any policy formation queries and holds relevant workplace publications.

Institute for the Study of Drug Dependence (ISDD)
1 Hatton Place
London EC1N 8ND
Tel: (071) 430 1993
Fax: (071) 404 4415
Founded: 1968
Contact: Information Officer

No other locations
Public library facilities
Workplace publications
Charge for some services/products

Offers library facilities which can help with any documentation regarding drugs and the workplace. The library materials and ISDD's own publications may be of use to the individual drug user.

Turning Point
New Loom House
101 Backchurch Lane
London E1 1LU
Tel: (071) 702 2300
Fax: (071) 702 1456
Founded: 1964
Contact: Mr John Marsden,
Workplace Services Consultant
No other locations
No public library facilities
No workplace publications
Charge for some services/products

Can assist in drafting or reviewing existing workplace policies with consultation on the content, scope and implementation and can provide training programmes for company staff on alcohol and drug problems. Will assist in locating relevant services and provides support and monitoring for the client organisation's own help service.

493 Project
493 Cambridge Heath Road
Bethnal Green
London E2 9BU
Tel: (071) 729 2070
Fax: –
Founded: 1990
Contact: Ms Rachel Grimstead,
Manager

No other locations
No public library facilities
No workplace publications
No charge for services/products

Offers clean injecting equipment and condoms to injecting drug users as well as primary health care, referrals to detoxification units and rehabilitation centres, counselling support and advice and information. Can also give pre- and post-HIV counselling and testing.

Other organisations
Action Against Allergy: **26**; Aquarius Action Projects: **24**; Bath Alcohol Advisory Centre:: **24**; Community Drug Project: **21**; The Libra Trust: **21**; National Association for Mental Health: **77**; The National College of Hypnosis and Psychotherapy: **43**; National Council of Psychotherapists and Hypnotherapy Register: **44**; Positively Women: **71**; Teetotallers Register: **25**.

EATING DISORDERS

Anorexia Anonymous
24 Westmoreland Road
Barnes
London SW13 9RY
Tel: (081) 748 3994
Fax: –
Founded: 1970
Contact: Mr J Hevesi, Founder
No other locations
No public library facilities
No workplace publications
No charge for services/products

Provides free advice and information on eating disorders, anorexia and bulimia nervosa. There is no set charge for treatment but a small contribution is required.

Eating Disorders Association
Sackville Place
44 Magdalen Street
Norwich
Norfolk NR3 1JE
Tel: (0603) 621414
Fax: (0603) 664915
Contact: Office
Numerous other locations
No public library facilities
Workplace publications
Charge for some services/products

Offers support to people with anorexia and bulimia nervosa and their families, provides information, offers training and education and tries to develop new thinking and understanding about eating disorders.

Overeaters Anonymous (OA)
Manor Garden Centre
6–9 Manor Gardens
London N7 6LA
Tel: (071) 275 8008
Founded: 1960
Contact: Office
102 other locations
No public library facilities
No workplace publications
No charge for services/products

Runs self-help groups which deal with all types of eating disorder. Please write to the above address, enclosing an SAE for details of nearest group, or telephone for details of London meetings and contacts.

Other organisations
The British Dietetic Association: **81**; The British Hypnotherapy Association: **76**; The British Nutrition Foundation: **81**; Brook Advisory Centres: **40**; Dr Jan de Winter Cancer Prevention Foundation: **36**; Just Ask Advisory and Counselling Service: **43**; The National College of Hypnosis and Psychotherapy: **43**; National Council of Psychotherapists and Hypnotherapy Register: **44**; National Society for Research into Allergy: **26**; Post Abortion Counselling Service: **98**; The Psychotherapy Centre: **44**; Society for Environmental Therapy: **57**; Women's Health: **97**.

The National Pure Water Association
Meridan
Caegoody Lane
Ellesmere
Shropshire SY12 9DW
Tel: (0691) 623015
Fax: –
Founded: 1960
Contact: Mr N Brugge, Secretary
No other locations
No public library facilities
No workplace publications
No charge for services/products

Opposes the use of public water supplies for the purpose of mass medication and promotes the protection of public water supplies from all forms of contamination.

National Society for Clean Air & Environmental Protection (NSCA)
136 North Street
Brighton BN1 7JF
Tel: (0273) 26313
Fax: (0273) 735802
Founded: 1898
Contact: information department
No other locations
Public library facilities
Workplace publications
Charge for some services/products

Provides an information service and leaflets on various aspects of pollution and health.

Noise Abatement Society
PO Box 8
Bromley
Kent BR2 0UH
Tel: (081) 460 3146
Fax: (081) 313 3314

Founded: 1959
Contact: Mr John Connell, Chairman
No other locations
No public library facilities
No workplace publications
Charge for some services/products

Can give information, advice and details of professional acoustics consultants to give on-site examination of problems and report on solutions. If necessary will give evidence in court and at public inquiries.

Society for Environmental Therapy (SET)
521 Foxhall Road
Ipswich
Suffolk IP3 8LW
Tel: –
Fax: –
Founded: 1980
Contact: Mrs H Davidson, Secretary
No other locations
No public library facilities
No workplace publications
Charge for some services/products

Listens to ideas about illness caused by food, air and water and to how people have coped with their illnesses and how we can find treatments without side effects. Membership open to anyone. All suggestions are published with a view to stimulating research on low technology treatment and environmental causes of illness.

Other organisations
Action Against Allergy: **26**; British Lung Foundation: **89**; City Centre Project Ltd: **107**; Food and Chemical Allergy Association: **26**; Health and Safety Advice Centre: **107**; London

Hazards Centre: **107**; The Medico 9
Organisation: **62**; National Asthma
Campaign: **89**; National Eczema
Society: **90**; National Society for
Research into Allergy: **26**; Royal
Society for the Prevention of
Accidents: **19**; Society for the
Prevention of Asbestosis and Indus-
trial Diseases: **29**.

British Epilepsy Association
Anstey House
40 Hanover Square
Leeds LS3 1BE
Tel: (0532) 439393
Fax: (0532) 428804
Founded: 1950
Contact: Ms Sue Cooper, PR Assistant
2 other locations
Public library facilities
Workplace publications
Charge for some services/products

Provides care in the community for people with epilepsy and has a range of services/publications on all aspects of the condition. The national information centre in Leeds provides an advice and information service to the public and professionals on all matters concerning epilepsy. Information available for employers and employees.

National Society for Epilepsy (NSE)
Chalfont Centre for Epilepsy
Chalfont St Peter
Bucks SL9 0RJ
Tel: (0494) 873991
Fax: (0494) 871927
Founded: 1892
Contact: Ms Catherine Dowds, Senior Health Education Officer
No other locations
No public library facilities
Workplace publications
Charge for some services/products

Has copies of *The standards of care* document produced by the Joint Epilepsy Council. This gives guidelines on good practice for employers. Information and advice available dealing with a wide variety of enquiries from employers and employees. Conferences about epilepsy and employment also held.

Other organisations
Bridges: **49**; National Council of Psychotherapists and Hypnotherapy Register: **44**.

ETHNIC-SPECIFIC ISSUES

Brent Sickle Cell and Thalassaemia Centre
Central Middlesex Hospital
Acton Lane
London NW10 7NS
Tel: (081) 453 2262
Fax: (081) 453 2680
Founded: 1979
*Contact: Miss Nina Patel, Senior
Counsellor*
No other locations
No public library facilities
Workplace publications
No charge for services/products

Answers questions and queries on sickle cell disease and thalassaemia and can refer people for counselling if required.

London Black Women Health Action Project
Globe Town Neighbourhood Centre
1 Cornwall Avenue
London. E2
Tel: (081) 980 3503
Fax: (081) 980 3503
Founded: 1982
*Contact: Ms Shamis Dirir,
Co-ordinator*
No other locations
Public library facilities
Workplace publications
Charge for some services/products

Holds workshops on various health topics in order to promote the health of black women in London, but will accept queries from anywhere in England. Can provide help, support and information to refugees and to circumcised women.

Sickle Cell Society
54 Station Road
London NW10 4UA
Tel: (081) 961 7795
Fax: (081) 961 8346
Founded: 1979
*Contact: Mr Peter Smith,
Administration Officer*
No other locations
No public library facilities
Workplace publications
No charge for services/products

Provides education, talks, seminars, and exhibitions on sickle cell disorders. Gives counselling for those in need and financial assistance for sufferers.

Sickle Cell and Thalassaemia Information Centre
St Leonard's Hospital
Nuttall Street
London N1 5LZ
Tel: (071) 739 8484
Fax: –
Founded: 1982
*Contact: Mrs Cora Woolcock, Senior
Counsellor*
No other locations
No public library facilities
Workplace publications
Charge for some services/products

Provides pre- and post-screening counselling, education, advice, information and support on sickle cell and thalassaemia disorders, with an open-door policy to the general public.

Help and support is also given to those needing emergency healthcare for complications resulting from these diseases, e.g. painful crises, strokes, jaundice etc. Can also refer people to other appropriate help sources.

Tay Sachs Screening Group (Manchester)
Research Centre
Royal Manchester Children's Hospital
Pendlebury
Manchester M27 1HA
Tel: (061) 794 4696 x 2384
Fax: –
Founded: 1982
Contact: Mr Alan Harris, Director
2 other locations
No public library facilities
Workplace publications
No charge for services/products

Maintains a resource list of physicians, genetic counsellors, therapists and other health and human service providers who are knowledgeable about the problems and circumstances of families with affected children. The parent peer group is co-ordinated by volunteers who are themselves parents of affected children. Members of the group have access to a directory of parents willing to be contacted by others confronted with the same or a similar situation.

United Kingdom Thalassaemia Society
107 Nightingale Lane
London N8 7QY
Tel: (081) 348 0437
Fax: (081) 348 2553
Founded: 1976
Contact: Ms Christine Pericleous,
Co-ordinator
2 other locations
No public library facilities

Workplace publications
No charge for services/products

Aims to educate people on the problems of thalassaemia and to offer counselling to sufferers and carriers. Will give lectures with the aid of slides and/or videos to explain thalassaemia in simple language to any group of people who wish to learn more about it. Brings together patients, families and well-wishers to exchange ideas and information.

Other organisations

Women's Health Information and Support Centre: **97**.

FIRST AID

British Red Cross
9 Grosvenor Crescent
London SW1X 7EJ
Tel: (071) 235 5454
Fax: (071) 245 6315
Founded: 1870
Contact: Mr Alan Taylor, Head of Development and Training
No other locations
No public library facilities
Workplace publications
Charge for some services/products

Runs courses on first aid at work; details from your local British Red Cross branch (see *Yellow pages*) or from the training department at the above address.

Coach and Bus First Aid Association
280 Old Marylebone Road
London NW1 5RJ
Tel: (071) 724 5600 x 21046
Fax: (071) 918 1146
Founded: 1932
Contact: Mr D A Crew, Honorary Secretary
No other locations
No public library facilities
Workplace publications
Charge for some services/products

Encourages employees of road passenger transport undertakings to become proficient in rendering first aid. Gives information and advice on first aid problems and statutory interpretations to any member company.

The Medico 9 Organisation
Park House
12 Old Portsmouth Road
Camberley
Surrey GU15 1JJ
Tel: (0276) 66280
Fax: –
Founded: 1979
Contact: Mr David Crew, Director
26 other locations
No public library facilities
Workplace publications
Charge for some services/products

Offers first aid training courses tailored to the individual workplace environment. With the main aim of providing a first aid and medical service to the general public, the organisation offers a 24-hour monitoring and communication service via the citizens' band radio network, and assistance to the professional services, and operates a major disaster policy which includes a list of available personnel and equipment.

St John Ambulance
1 Grosvenor Crescent
London SW1X 7EF
Tel: (071) 235 5231
Fax: (071) 235 0796
Founded: 1877
Contact: Mr John Mills, Director of Public Relations
No other locations
Public library facilities
Workplace publications
Charge for some services/products

Assists in first aid provision for employers, giving advice and assistance as required. Can answer queries on first aid requirements in relation to those of the Health and Safety Executive.

Other organisations

British Diabetic Association: **81**; British Epilepsy Association: **59**; British Heart Foundation: **69**; Health and Safety Advice Centre: **107**; London Black Women Health Action Project: **60**; London Central Young Men's Christian Association: **86**; The National Association of Laryngec-tomee Clubs: **38**; National Asthma Campaign: **89**; Royal Society for the Prevention of Accidents: **19**.

FOOT HEALTH

Foot Health Council
c/o Wessex School of Podiatry
Dept F
7 Archers Road
Southampton
Hants SO1 2LQ
Tel: –
Fax: (0703) 230944
Founded: 1979
Contact: The Honorary Secretary
No other locations
No public library facilities
Workplace publications
Charge for some services/products

Yearly guidelines produced relating to relevant campaigns. Answers queries relating to feet and shoes through direct contact or referral to an expert.

The Golden Shoe Club (Safety Footwear) Ltd
PO Box 11
Holt
Norfolk
NR25 6RL
Tel: (0263) 712721
Fax: (0263) 713767
Founded: 1963
Contact: Mr John Morrish, Secretary
No other locations
No public library facilities
Workplace publications
Charge for some services/products

Represents the leading manufacturers and distributors of safety footwear made under BSI licence and aims to reduce the number of industrial injuries through the wearing of genuine safety footwear. This message is given through educational programmes, booklets, videos and demonstrations to show the value of safety footwear. Free personal accident insurance cover is given to wearers of safety footwear supplied by all sponsors of the club which also operates an award scheme for escapers of serious foot injuries through the wearing of members' safety footwear.

Institute of Chiropodists
91 Lord Street
Southport
Merseyside PR8 1SA
Tel: (0704) 546141
Fax: (0704) 500477
Founded: 1938
Contact: Mr JA Kirkham, Secretary
No other locations
No public library facilities
Workplace publications
Charge for some services/products

A professional body serving the chiropody profession. Provides names and addresses of local chiropodists by telephone or written request.

Society of Chiropodists
53 Welbeck Street
London W1M 7HE
Tel: (071) 486 3381
Fax: (071) 935 6359
Founded: 1945
Contact: Mr MHP Collins, Assistant Secretary (Industrial Relations)
No other locations
No public library facilities
Workplace publications
Charge for some services/products

Develops and promotes policies on foot care, health and management education and produces educational leaflets. It can also give information on foot problems and sources of treatment.

Solemates

46 Gordon Road
Chingford
London E4 6BU
Tel: (081) 524 2423
Fax: –
Founded: 1976
Contact: Ms Ann Cross, Chairman
No other locations
No public library facilities
No workplace publications
Charge for some services/products

An organisation for people with different-sized feet or only one foot. It offers a partnering service to cut personal costs. Information on manufacturers and suppliers of odd sizes. Can occasionally supply footwear via its membership of over 3,000 people.

Other organisations

British Diabetic Association: **48**; Disabled Living Foundation: **50**; The Medico 9 Organisation: **62**; National Eczema Society: **90**; The Psoriasis Association: **90**; Royal Society for the Prevention of Accidents: **19**; Sickle Cell and Thalassaemia Information Centre: **60**.

HEARING

Breakthrough – Deaf-Hearing Integration
Charles W Gillett Centre
998 Bristol Road
Selly Oak
Birmingham B29 6LE
Tel: (021) 472 6447
Fax: (021) 471 4368
Founded: 1971
*Contact: Ms Gillian Winstanley,
Publications Co-ordinator*
2 other locations
Public library facilities
No workplace publications
No charge for services/products

Integrates deaf and hearing people in social activities and practical projects. Total communiation workshops and courses increase deaf awareness. Tele-computing gives training in tele-communications and computer skills. Information and resources on deafness are available in centres and mobile units, for which a donation is usually asked. Text telephone on (021) 471 1001.

British Association of the Hard of Hearing (BAHOH)
7-11 Armstrong Road
London W3 7JL
Tel: (081) 742 1110
Fax: (081) 742 9043
Founded: 1947
*Contact: Mrs E Jones, Welfare
Administrator*
No other locations
No public library facilities
Workplace publications
Charge for some services/products

Can provide information on equipment available to assist the deaf and hard of hearing to either continue in, or obtain, employment. Can offer advice and information on any aspect of hearing impairment in the workplace, including individual cases.

British Tinnitus Association
Room 6
14-18 West Bar Green
Sheffield S1 2DA
Tel: –
Fax: –
Founded: 1979
*Contact: Miss M Scarr, Honorary
Secretary*
No other locations
No public library facilities
Workplace publications
Charge for some services/products

Helps to implement and form self-help groups which provide mutual support and varying degrees of counselling.

Council for the Development of Communication with Deaf People (CACDP)
Pelaw House
School of Education
University of Durham
DH1 1TA
Tel: (091) 374 3607
Fax: (091) 374 3605
Founded: 1982
*Contact: Mr TS Simpson, Chief
Executive*
1 other location
No public library facilities
Workplace publications
Charge for some services/products

Promotes training and conducts examinations in communication skills used by deaf people, and between deaf and hearing people.

Provides information on the use and availability of interpreters, the development of communication skills in sign language, lip speaking and communicating with deaf blind people.

The above telephone number is for voice and minicom; minicom answering machine is available on (091) 374 3614.

Hearing Dogs for the Deaf
The Training Centre
London Road
Lewknor
Oxford OX9 5RY
Tel: (0844) 353898
Fax: (0844) 353099
Founded: 1982
Contact: Mr AG Blunt, Director
No other locations
No public library facilities
Workplace publications
No charge for services/products

Trains dogs to act as the ears of the profoundly deaf or hard of hearing.

International Audiology Society
16 Nithsdale Road
Weston Super Mare
Avon BS23 4JR
Tel: –
Fax: –
Founded: 1970
Contact: Mrs EA Crellin, Chairman
No other locations
No public library facilities
Workplace publications
Charge for some services/products

Offers information, advice and counselling to those with hearing and speech problems. Correspondence courses available. Visits by arrangement.

Link, The British Centre for Deafened People
19 Hartfield Road
Eastbourne
East Sussex BN21 2AR
Tel: (0323) 638230
Fax: –
Founded: 1972
Contact: Dr L Gailey, Director
No other locations
No public library facilities
Workplace publications
Charge for some services/products

Runs short-term residential rehabilitation courses for people who become profoundly deaf as adults. Aims to improve communication, rebuild social confidence and increase personal adjustment.

National Association of Deafened People (NADP)
103 Heath Road
Widnes
Cheshire WA8 7NU
Tel: (051) 424 3977
Fax: (051) 420 7316
Founded: 1984
Contact: Mr GT Brown, Honorary Membership Secretary
No other locations
No public library facilities
Workplace publications
Charge for some services/products

Can advise on rehabilitation and future employment and training for employees who become deaf. Can also give advice on the general treatment of deaf employees and the recruitment and selection of people with hearing impairments. Deals with problems on all aspects of profound/total acquired hearing loss. Encourages the formation of local support groups and publishes a quarterly newsletter.

National Deaf-Blind League
18 Rainbow Court
Paston Ridings
Peterborough PE4 6UP
Tel: (0733) 573511
Fax: (0733) 325353
Founded: 1928
Contact: Ms Ann Barnett, Chief Executive
2 other locations
No public library facilities
No workplace publications
Charge for some services/products

Gives practical advice and financial assistance to members, organises conferences, seminars and communication courses nationally, promotes public awareness and negotiates with local and central government to provide better services and facilities for the deaf-blind.
Charges for services vary depending on the circumstances; in some cases they will be waived completely.

The Sympathetic Hearing Scheme (SHS)
7-11 Armstrong Road
London W3 7JL
Tel: (081) 740 4447
Fax: (081) 742 9043
Founded: 1982
Contact: Mr Richard Gray, Co-ordinator
No other locations
No public library facilities
Workplace publications
Charge for some services/products

Offers information and advice on policy regarding communication with deaf and hard-of-hearing customers or clients and can set up staff training on this subject. Can also provide the above services in relation to dealing with specific problems.

Other organisations
The British Deaf Association: **70**; Centre for Accessible Environments: **50**; Health and Safety Advice Centre: **107**; The National College of Hypnosis and Psychotherapy: **43**; National Society for Research into Allergy: **26**; Noise Abatement Society: **57**; Royal Society for the Prevention of Accidents: **19**; Society for the Prevention of Asbestosis and Industrial Diseases: **29**.

British Heart Foundation
14 Fitzhardinge Street
London W1H 4DH
Tel: (071) 935 0185
Fax: (071) 486 1273
Founded: 1961
Contact: Ms Heather Waring,
Education Manager
9 other locations
No public library facilities
Workplace publications
No charge for services/products

Will advise companies on heart health within the workplace and give factual information to help them formulate policies. Booklets, leaflets and videos are available to anyone on specific problems relating to heart and circulatory diseases.

Coronary Prevention Group
102 Gloucester Place
London W1H 3DA
Tel: (071) 935 2889
Fax: (071) 487 5692
Founded: 1979
Contact: Ms Julia Robinson,
Commercial Manager
No other locations
No public library facilities
Workplace publications
Charge for some services/products

Publishes the *Your heart* series of booklets covering healthy eating, cholesterol, smoking, stress, blood pressure and exercise plus factsheets and other publications. Bulk discounts are available.

Family Heart Association
Wesley House
7 High Street
Kidlington
Oxford OX5 2DS
Tel: (08675) 70292
Fax: (08675) 70295
Founded: 1984
Contact: Mr Don Steele, Director
No other locations
No public library facilities
Workplace publications
Charge for some services/products

Can provide on-site risk factor screening including cholesterol testing as well as giving advice on canteen and restaurant menus and personal dietary advice.

Other organisations
The British Dietetic Association: **81**; Dr Jan de Winter Cancer Prevention Foundation: **36**; London Black Women Health Action Project: **60**; Marie Stopes International: **40**; The National College of Hypnosis and Psychotherapy: **43**; Women's Health Concern Ltd: **99**.

HIV/AIDS

The British Deaf Association (BDA)
38 Victoria Place
Carlisle
Cumbria CA1 1HU
Tel: (0228) 48844
Fax: (0228) 41420
Founded: 1890
Contact: Ms Lilian Lawson, Head of Administration
2 other locations
No public library facilities
No workplace publications
Charge for some services/products

Provides information and undertakes welfare work to help deaf people. Promotes the use of British Sign Language and runs a network of branches. AIDS Ahead is part of the BDA and deals specifically with any health issue in relation to deaf people.

For voice and minicom users, telephone (0228) 28719.

For information on AIDS and any other health issue please contact Mr Peter Jackson at AIDS Ahead, 144 London Road, Northwich, Cheshire, CW9 5HH. Telephone: (0606) 330472 for 24 hour text phone, and (0606) 47047 for 24 hour voice phone.

HEA National HIV Prevention Information Service (NHPIS)
82-86 Seymour Place
London W1H 5DB
Tel: (071) 724 7993
Fax: (071) 723 7688
Founded: 1990
Contact: Ms Kristina Bird, Information Officer
No other locations
No public library facilities
No workplace publications

No charge for services/products

A national enquiry and referral service for those working in HIV prevention, education and training. Can provide employers with information about workplace specific infection control and official guidelines about employment practices as well as signposting to other helpful organisations.

This service is funded by the Health Education Authority (see section on Health Education Authority services to the workplace for full details of the HIV/AIDS and sexual health programme).

Immunity Legal Centre
260a Kilburn Lane
London W10 4BA
Tel: (081) 968 8909
Fax: (081) 968 6496
Founded: 1985
Contact: Ms Susie Craig, Administrator
No other locations
No public library facilities
Workplace publications
Charge for some services/products

Free legal advice, information and/or representation for anyone affected by HIV and AIDS. Main areas of work surround immigration, housing, wills, insurance, health and employment, but also welfare rights. Services available by telephone, by appointment at the centre or home/hospital visits.

The centre also runs advice sessions at The Landmark, The London Lighthouse, Body Positive and The Riverhouse.

For publications please telephone (081) 968 6507.

London Lighthouse

111-117 Lancaster Road
London W11 1QT
Tel: (071) 792 1200
Fax: (071) 229 1258
Founded: 1986
Contact: Mr Ben McKnight,
Information Officer
No other locations
Public library facilities
Workplace publications
Charge for some services/products

Runs courses and seminars with policy building components on HIV/AIDS. Advice and support to anyone living with, or affected by, HIV/AIDS. This includes counselling, peer support, creative and complementary therapies, training and education, residential and daycare, community services and welfare rights and advice.

Library facilities available to those who use the service.

National AIDS Manual (NAM)

Unit 407
Brixton Enterprise Centre
London SW9 8EJ
Tel: (071) 737 1846
Fax: (071) 737 6190
Founded: 1988
Contact: Mr Peter Scott, Editor
No other locations
No public library facilities
Workplace publications
Charge for some services/products

Comprehensive guidance and advice is contained in the manual relating to all issues of HIV/AIDS. Particular policy issues include employing people with HIV/AIDS, testing for HIV, infection control and health education. The manual also provides immediate information for questions relating to the prevention of transmission of HIV, and to the needs of people living with HIV/AIDS. There is also a comprehensive directory of all HIV services in the country from which further advice can be sought.

National AIDS Trust (NAT)

14th Floor
Euston Tower
286 Euston Road
London NW1 3DN
Tel: (071) 383 4246
Fax: (071) 383 5165
Founded: 1987
Contact: Ms Vanessa Hardy,
Development Officer – Employers'
Initiative
No other locations
No public library facilities
Workplace publications
No charge for services/products

Can advise on drafting workplace policies and recommend local organisations able to help, particularly with education programmes. Can also answer specific queries on HIV/AIDS, recommending specialist advisers where necessary.

Positively Women

5 Sebastian Street
London EC1V 0HE
Tel: (071) 490 5515
Fax: (071) 490 1690
Founded: 1987
Contact: Ms Lesley Foote,
Administrator
No other locations
No public library facilities
Workplace publications
Charge for some services/products

Aims to provide confidential, free, practical and emotional support to women with HIV. It offers telephone and one-to-one counselling as well as support groups.

St Bartholomew's Hospital Worried Well Service

51-53 Bartholomew Close
London EC1A 7BE
Tel: (071) 601 7357
Fax: (071) 726 4248
Founded: 1987
Contact: Mr Bill Nelson, HIV/AIDS Counsellor
No other locations
No public library facilities
Workplace publications
Charge for some services/products

Willing to give policy advice to employers for the benefit of HIV infected employees. The Worried Well Service is a clinic for people concerned about HIV infection and AIDS and provides counselling and HIV testing. The service is confidential, and same day results are available by arrangement. Please ring for an appointment.

If HIV testing is for insurance or visa purposes there will be a charge.

Other organisations

British Association for Counselling: **42**; Brook Advisory Centres: **40**; Cancer Relief Macmillan Fund: **36**; Community Drug Project: **21**; Family Planning Association: **40**; Haemophilia Society: **75**; Hungerford Drug Project: **54**; Institute for the Study of Drug Dependence: **54**; Lesbian and Gay Bereavement Project: **31**; London Black Women Health Action Project: **60**; London Central Young Men's Christian Association: **86**; Marie Curie Cancer Care: **38**; National Council of Psychotherapists and Hypnotherapy Register: **44**; Outset – Action on Disability: **52**; Release: **21**; Royal Society for the Prevention of Accidents: **19**; The Samaritans: **45**; St John Ambulance: **62**; Turning Point: **55**; Women's Health: **97**; Women's Health Information and Support Centre: **97**; 493 Project: **55**.

HYPERTENSION

There are no organisations listed in this directory which deal specifically with hypertension as their main area of work. However, the following organisations can provide help and/or information in this field. For full details please refer to their entry on the page indicated below.

The British Dietetic Association: **81**; British Heart Foundation: **69**; The British Hypnotherapy Association: **76**; Coronary Prevention Group: **69**; Dr Jan de Winter Cancer Prevention Foundation: **36**; The National College of Hypnosis and Psychotherapy: **43**; National Council of Psychotherapists and Hypnotherapy Register: **44**; National Society for Research into Allergy: **26**.

ME (MYALGIC ENCEPHALOMYELITIS)

M E Action Campaign
PO Box 1302
Wells
Somerset BA5 2WE
Tel: (0749) 670799
Fax: –
Founded: 1987
Contact: Ms Angela Henderson,
Director
No other locations
No public library facilities
Workplace publications
Charge for some services/products

Offers a comprehensive range of literature aimed at educating primarily people with ME, but also employers, doctors, family and others about how to cope with ME. Free factsheet, details of literature and membership services available on request with a large SAE.

Other organisations
Action Against Allergy: **26**; Cystitis and Candida: **97**; National Society for Research into Allergy: **26**; Society for Environmental Therapy: **57**.

MEN'S HEALTH: GENERAL

There are no organisations listed in this directory which deal specifically with general male health issues as their main area of work. However, the following organisations can provide help and/or information in this field. For full details please refer to their entry on the page indicated opposite.

British Dental Health Foundation: **47**; The British Hypnotherapy Association: **76**; European Foundation for the Improvement of Living and Working Conditions: **107**; Family Planning Association: **40**; Health and Safety Advice Centre: **107**; The Herpes Association: **90**; Just Ask Advisory and Counselling Service: **43**; Marie Stopes International: **40**; National Council of Psychotherapists and Hypnotherapy Register: **44**; Post Abortion Counselling Service: **98**; The Psoriasis Association: **90**; The Psychotherapy Centre: **44**; St John Ambulance: **62**; Save Our Sons: **38**.

MEN'S HEALTH: HAEMOPHILIA

Haemophilia Society
123 Westminster Bridge Road
London SE1 7HR
Tel: (071) 928 2020
Fax: (071) 620 1416
Founded: 1950
Contact: Mr David Watters, General Secretary
No other locations

No public library facilities
Workplace publications
No charge for services/products

Provides advice and information to employers regarding the treatment of people with haemophilia in the workplace and their integration with the normal workforce.

MEN'S HEALTH: VASECTOMY

There are no organisations listed in this directory which deal specifically with vasectomy as their main area of work. However, the following organisations can provide help and/or information in this field. For full details please refer to their entry on the page indicated below.

British Pregnancy Advisory Service: **98**; Brook Advisory Centres: **40**; Family Planning Association: **40** Marie Stopes International: **40**; The Medical Education Trust: **41**

MENTAL HEALTH

The British Hypnotherapy Association (BHA)

1 Wythburn Place
Westminster
London W1H 5WL
Tel: (071) 723 4443
Fax: –
Founded: 1958
Contact: The Secretary
No other locations
Public library facilities
Workplace publications
Charge for some services/products

Offers advice to employers on the emotional health of their staff and can refer people on to trained practitioners who can help them to resolve their emotional problems, marital difficulties, psychogenic disorders, psychosexual problems, alcoholism, migraine etc.

Library available to friends and members of the BHA only.

Depressives Associated

PO Box 1022
London SE1 7QB
Tel: (081) 760 0544
Fax: –
Founded: 1979
Contact: Ms Doris Kempe, Secretary
No other locations
No public library facilities
No workplace publications
Charge for some services/products

Offers information, support and understanding for people with depression and for relatives who want to help. Members receive a quarterly newsletter. There is a pen-friend scheme and personal replies to any letters. Leaflets are available on related subjects. Help given in the establishment of local self-help groups.

Fellowship of Depressives Anonymous (FDA)

36 Chestnut Avenue
Beverley
North Humberside HU17 9QU
Tel: (0482) 860619
Fax: –
Founded: 1973
Contact: Mr Geoff Heath,
Membership Secretary
20 other locations
No public library facilities
No workplace publications
Charge for some services/products

For people who have, or have had, depression and who wish to support and encourage recovery in others through a quarterly newsletter, pen-friend scheme and local support groups. Offers support and information to those setting up local groups. Telephone queries to Geoff Heath, letters to Pat Freya.

Manic Depression Fellowship

13 Rosslyn Road
Twickenham
Middlesex TW1 2AR
Tel: (081) 892 2811
Fax: –
Founded: 1983
Contact: Ms Barbara Waters, Director
No other locations
No public library facilities
Workplace publications
Charge for some services/products

Provides information about manic

depression and the needs of those with manic depression in an employment setting. Also provides an introduction to self-help groups and carers plus a pen-friend scheme. Membership includes a quarterly newsletter. For free information pack, please write or telephone.

National Association for Mental Health (MIND)
22 Harley Street
London W1N 2ED
Tel: (071) 637 0741
Fax: (071) 323 0061
Founded: 1946
Contact: MIND
7 other locations
Public library facilities
Workplace publications
Charge for some services/products

MIND's policy department has written an employment pack promoting good practice in the workplace and is willing to be consulted on policy formation on issues such as mental health discrimination and promotion in the workplace. The MIND information line is open every weekday between 10–12.30pm and 2–4.30pm to give information to individuals or organisations. Legal department will provide relevant legal advice.

Sanity
Robina
The Chase
Ringwood
Hants BH24 2AN
Tel: (0425) 479880
Fax: –
Founded: 1973
Contact: Mrs Margery Hall, Chairman

2 other locations
Public library facilities
Workplace publications
No charge for services/products

Aims to bring relief to persons who are suffering from mental illness, an illness believed by Sanity to be primarily of chemical and genetic origin. To this end it collects worldwide literature on biophysical, biochemical and nutritional factors in mental health. Practical help is given through dietary and other advice.

Schizophrenia Association of Great Britain (SAGB)
International Schizophrenia Centre
Bryn Hyfryd
The Crescent
Bangor
Gwynedd LL57 2AG
Tel: (0248) 354048
Fax: –
Founded: 1970
Contact: Mrs Gwynneth Hemmings, Director
No other locations
No public library facilities
Workplace publications
No charge for services/products

Helps people with schizophrenia and their families through telephone and postal help lines, distributes information sheets and newsletters to enquirers and members and carries out major research into the causes of schizophrenia. Callers to the centre are advised to make an appointment.

Other organisations
Anorexia Anonymous: **56**; Association for Post Natal Illness: **101**; Bath

Alcohol Advisory Centre: **24**; Bridges: **49**; British Association of Psychotherapists: **42**; British Epilepsy Association: **59**; Eating Disorders Association: **56**; Helen Arkell Dyslexia Centre: **93**; Identity Counselling Service: **43**; Just Ask Advisory and Counselling Service: **43**; Lesbian and Gay Bereavement Project: **31**; London Black Women Health Action Project: **60**; The National College of Hypnosis and Psychotherapy: **43**; National Council of Psychotherapists and Hypnotherapy Register: **44**; Outset – Action on Disability: **52**; Portia Trust: **44**; The Psoriasis Association: **90**; The Samaritans: **45**; Stillbirth and Neonatal Death Society: **32**; The Topaz Line: **45**; Turning Point: **55**; Westminster Pastoral Foundation: **45**.

The Migraine Trust
45 Great Ormond Street
London WC1N 3HZ
Tel: (071) 278 2676
Fax: (071) 831 5174
Founded: 1965
Contact: Mrs Ann Rush, Deputy Director
No other locations
No public library facilities
Workplace publications
No charge for services/products

Supports people with migraine by helping to fund clinics, by providing a helpline and with quarterly newsletters which detail new drugs and self-help ideas etc. People with migraine can attend the clinics after referral from their GP.

Funds research at hospitals and universities worldwide and holds an international migraine symposium every 2 years.

Other organisations
Action Against Allergy: **26**; The British Hypnotherapy Association: **76**; The National College of Hypnosis and Psychotherapy: **43**; National Council of Psychotherapists and Hypnotherapy Register: **44**; National Society for Research into Allergy: **26**; The Psychotherapy Centre: **44**; Society for Environmental Therapy: **57**.

MULTIPLE SCLEROSIS

Action and Research for Multiple Sclerosis (ARMS)
4a Chapel Hill
Stansted
Essex CM24 8AG
Tel: (0279) 815553
Fax: (0279) 647179
Founded: 1975
Contact: Mr B Mather,
Administration Manager
80 other locations
No public library facilities
Workplace publications
Charge for some services/products

Provides information on the ways in which work capability can be influenced by MS and on coping with it in the workplace. Gives consultations on the practicalities of successful employment of people with disabilities with MS in specific types of work.

The Multiple Sclerosis Society of Great Britain and Northern Ireland
25 Effie Road
London SW6 1EE
Tel: (071) 736 6267
Fax: (071) 736 9861
Founded: 1953
Contact: Mr John Walford, General
Secretary
370 other locations
No public library facilities
Workplace publications
No charge for services/products

Both direct assistance and information is available from the headquarters offices in London, Edinburgh and Belfast, and from local branches. For details contact the London headquarters.

Other organisations
Disabled Living Foundation: 50.

The British Dietetic Association
7th Floor
Elizabeth House
22 Suffolk Street
Queensway
Birmingham B1 1LS
Tel: (021) 643 5483
Fax: (021) 633 4399
Founded: 1936
Contact: Miss V Jones, Organising
Secretary
No other locations
No public library facilities
Workplace publications
Charge for some services/products

Can identify specialist/freelance state registered dietitians who will act as consultants on all aspects of workplace nutrition, including the evaluation of existing services and programmes for improvement. Problems and/or queries will be directed to the appropriate state registered dietitian as the association itself does not offer a problem solving service.

The British Nutrition Foundation (BNF)
15 Belgrave Square
London SW1X 8PG
Tel: (071) 235 4904
Fax: (071) 235 5336
Founded: 1967
Contact: Mr JP Wood, Secretary
No other locations
No public library facilities
Workplace publications
Charge for some services/products

Maintains a comprehensive nutritional information database and staff scientists are available for enquiries and data

searches. A full consultancy and advice service can be provided.

Staff education programmes about food, nutrition and health can be arranged. General advice is provided but individual dietary advice is not.

The Food Commission
88 Old Street
London EC1V 9AR
Tel: (071) 253 9513
Fax: (071) 608 1279
Founded: 1985
Contact: Ms Martine Drake,
Information Officer
No other locations
Public library facilities
Workplace publications
Charge for some services/products

Offers consultancy services and is experienced in developing and implementing food policies. The commission's quarterly magazine and other publications provide information on food quality, safety and policy.

Other organisations
Action Against Allergy: **26**; Action and Research for Multiple Sclerosis: **80**; Anorexia Anonymous: **56**; British Dental Health Foundation: **47**; British Diabetic Association: **48**; British Heart Foundation: **69**; Coronary Prevention Group: **69**; Cystitis and Candida: **97**; Dr Jan de Winter Cancer Prevention Foundation: **36**; Family Heart Association: **69**; The Herpes Association: **90**; La Leche League (Great Britain): **102**; London Black Women Health Action Project: **60**; London Central Young Men's

Christian Association: **86**; ME Action Campaign: **74**; National Council of Psychotherapists and Hypnotherapy Register: **44**; National Eczema Society: **90**; National Society for Research into Allergy: **26**; Premenstrual Society: **106**; Sanity: **77**; Sickle Cell and Thalassaemia Information Centre: **60**; Society for Environmental Therapy: **57**; Women's Health Concern Ltd: **99**.

OSTEOPOROSIS

National Osteoporosis Society (NOS)
PO Box 10
Radstock
Bath
Avon BA3 3YB
Tel: (0761) 432472
Fax: (0761) 437903
Founded: 1986
Contact: Mrs Vanessa Collier, Deputy Director
32 other locations
No public library facilities
No workplace publications
Charge for some services/products

Offers information on osteoporosis to those with osteoporosis, health professionals and the general public. The society has a medical board of over 40 leading doctors and consultants to advise on all aspects of the disease.

Other organisations
Cystitis and Candida: **97**; Marie Stopes International: **40**; Women's Health Concern Ltd: **99**.

PERSONAL HYGIENE

There are no organisations listed in this directory which deal specifically with personal hygiene as their main area of work. However, the following organisations can provide help and/or information in this field. For full details please refer to their entry on the page indicated below.

British Dental Health Foundation: **47**; British Red Cross: **62**; Cystitis and Candida: **97**; Dr Jan de Winter Cancer Prevention Foundation: **36**; The Herpes Association: **90**; London Black Women Health Action Project: **60**; Royal Society for the Prevention of Accidents: **19**; Sickle Cell and Thalassaemia Information Centre: **60**; Women's Health Concern Ltd: **99**.

Action on Phobias (AOP)

8 The Avenue
Eastbourne
Sussex BN21 0BY
Tel: –
Fax: (0323) 422468
Founded: 1980
Contact: Dr D Hodgson, Clinical Director
15 other locations
No public library facilities
Workplace publications
Charge for some services/products

Provides free information on phobias and general anxiety conditions plus home-based audio cassette treatment programmes for which a small charge is made. Can assist in setting up self-help groups.

Phobic Action

Claybury Grounds
Manor Road
Woodford Green
Essex IG8 8PR
Tel: (081) 559 2551
Fax: –
Founded: 1977
Contact: Mr K Sell, Director
No other locations
No public library facilities
No workplace publications
Charge for some services/products

Assists people in recovery from anxiety-related problems and offers literature, self-help groups and telephone help line support on (0452) 856021 and (081) 559 2459.

Other organisations

Association for Post Natal Illness: **101**; British Dental Health Foundation: **47**; The British Hypnotherapy Association: **76**; Dr Jan de Winter Cancer Prevention Foundation: **36**; National Association for Mental Health: **77**; The National College of Hypnosis and Psychotherapy: **43**; National Council of Psychotherapists and Hypnotherapy Register: **44**; The Psychotherapy Centre: **44**; The Topaz Line: **45**.

PHYSICAL ACTIVITY

The Central Council of Physical Recreation (CCPR)
Francis House
Francis Street
London SW1P 1DE
Tel: (071) 828 3163
Fax: (071) 630 8820
Founded: 1937
Contact: Mr Stephen Saddler,
Technical Officer
No other locations
No public library facilities
Workplace publications
Charge for some services/products

Can deal with any sport or recreational query anywhere in the UK.

London Central Young Men's Christian Association (CENTYMCA)
112 Great Russell Street
London WC1B 3NQ
Tel: (071) 637 8131
Fax: (071) 436 1278
Founded: 1844
Contact: Mr Hedley Picton, Executive
Director
No other locations
No public library facilities
Workplace publications
Charge for some services/products

There are four separate operations within the London Central YMCA:
- Y touring – a theatre in health education company which can provide workplace workshops on HIV/AIDS and other health issues
- Just Ask – an advice and counselling service
- Training and development – teacher training in health related exercise

- Membership based club operation – offers opportunities to develop healthy practices in all dimensions

Sports Council
16 Upper Woburn Place
London WC1H 0QP
Tel: (071) 388 1277
Fax: (071) 383 5740
Founded: 1972
Contact: The Information Centre
9 other locations
Public library facilities
Workplace publications
Charge for some services/products

An information service is available 9am–5pm Monday to Friday to give information on many aspects of sport from facility design to participation. A reference library is available and sports council publications can be purchased.

Other organisations
British Heart Foundation: **69**; Coronary Prevention Group: **69**; Dr Jan de Winter Cancer Prevention Foundation: **36**; Family Heart Association: **69**; London Black Women Health Action Project: **60**; The National Association of Laryngestomee Clubs: **38**; Sickle Cell and Thalassaemia Information Centre: **60**.

Centre for Policy on Ageing (CPA)
25-31 Ironmonger Row
London EC1V 3QP
Tel: (071) 253 1787
Fax: (071) 490 4206
Founded: 1947
Contact: Library
No other locations
Public library facilities
Workplace publications
Charge for some services/products

CPA's library and series of published reports give background on old age/social gerontology for formulating policies affecting older people. The library and information service is able to deal with subject queries and supply reading lists on issues affecting older people.

The Pre-Retirement Association of Great Britain and Northern Ireland (PRA)
Nodus Centre
University Campus
Guildford
Surrey GU2 5RX
Tel: (0483) 39323
Fax: (0483) 38991
Founded: 1964
Contact: Mr Bernard Ring, General Secretary
No other locations
No public library facilities
Workplace publications
Charge for some services/products

Offers help and advice to employers wishing to offer or improve on their retirement preparation education, and is a national resource for information, ideas and the practice of retirement preparation. Runs courses and seminars for people approaching retirement but does not advocate particular products or services.

Reach
89 Southwark Street
London SE1 0HD
Tel: (071) 928 0452
Fax: (071) 928 0798
Founded: 1979
Contact: Mr Keith Galpin, Development Manager
No other locations
No public library facilities
Workplace publications
No charge for services/products

Finds part-time, expenses-only jobs for retired business or other professional men and women who want to use their skills to help voluntary organisations with charitable aims. The service is free.

The University of the Third Age (U3A)
U3A National Office
1 Stockwell Green
London SW9 9JF
Tel: (071) 737 2541
Fax: –
Contact: U3A
120 other locations
No public library facilities
No workplace publications
Charge for some services/products

Provides opportunities for all kinds of constructive activities and involves older adults in the creation and organisation of their own programmes. Each local group has its own programme. Languages, literary and artistic studies are popular but most U3As have walking groups, and across the whole country study groups focus on approximately 200 different topics.

Other organisations

Disabled Living Foundation: **50**; Dr Jan de Winter Cancer Prevention Foundation: **36**; The National College of Hypnosis and Psychotherapy: **43**.

British Lung Foundation (BLF)
8 Peterborough Mews
London SW6 3BL
Tel: (071) 371 7704
Fax: (071) 371 7705
Founded: 1985
Contact: Ms Christa M Paxton,
Director
3 other locations
No public library facilities
No workplace publications
No charge for services/products

Provides fact sheets on request on a variety of lung-related issues which could be used in health and safety or social and community policy making. Runs the Breathe Easy Club: a network for people living with a chronic lung disease.

National Asthma Campaign (NAC)
Providence House
Providence Place
London N1 0NT
Tel: (071) 226 2260
Fax: (071) 704 0740
Founded: 1990
Contact: Ms Fiona McLean,
Information Officer
No other locations
No public library facilities
Workplace publications
Charge for services/products

Provides information about asthma and all aspects of living with it. The asthma helpline is staffed by nurses with additional asthma training. The helpline is open from 1-9pm weekdays, on (0345) 010203. There is a network of local groups run by volunteers with personal experience of asthma.

Other organisations
Action Against Allergy: **26**; The British Hypnotherapy Association: **76**; Food and Chemical Allergy Association: **26**; Health and Safety Advice Centre: **107**; Mobility Trust: **50**; The National College of Hypnosis and Psychotherapy: **43**; National Council of Psychotherapists and Hypnotherapy Register: **44**; National Pollen and Hayfever Bureau: **26**; National Society for Clean Air and Environmental Protection: **57**; National Society for Research into Allergy: **26**; The Psychotherapy Centre: **44**; Royal Society for the Prevention of Accidents: **19**; Society for Environmental Therapy: **57**; Society for the Prevention of Asbestosis and Industrial Diseases: **29**; Steroid Aid Group: **28**.

SKIN COMPLAINTS

The Herpes Association
41 North Road
London N7 9DP
Tel: (071) 607 9661
Fax: –
Founded: 1982
Contact: Mr Michael Wolfe, Executive Officer
No other locations
Public library facilities
Workplace publications
Charge for some services/products

Acts as an umbrella organisation providing information and advice to those who have primary and recurrent attacks of herpes; liaising with doctors, co-ordinating support groups for members, responding to media coverage about herpes and promoting increased public awareness about the condition. All services are free of charge. Helpline on (071) 609 9061.

National Eczema Society (NES)
4 Tavistock Place
London WC1H 9RA
Tel: (071) 388 4097
Fax: (071) 713 0733
Founded: 1975
Contact: Ms Julie Braithwaite, Information Officer
No other locations
No public library facilities
Workplace publications
Charge for some services/products

Produces a wide range of publications including an information pack and booklets for professionals. Enquiries by telephone and letter are welcome.

The Psoriasis Association
7 Milton Street
Northampton NN2 7JG
Tel: (0604) 711129
Fax: (0604) 792894
Founded: 1968
Contact: Mrs Linda Henley, National Secretary
No other locations
No public library facilities
Workplace publications
No charge for services/products

Welcomes enquiries and offers help, where appropriate, to those who may have employment problems related to their psoriatic state. Also offers information and advice to any interested party.

Other organisations
British Association for Immediate Care: **19**; The British Hypnotherapy Association: **76**; La Leche League (Great Britain): **102**; National Council of Psychotherapists and Hypnotherapy Register: **44**; National Society for Research into Allergy: **26**; The Psychotherapy Register: **44**.

SMOKING

Action on Smoking and Health (ASH)
109 Gloucester Place
London W1H 3PH
Tel: (071) 935 3519
Fax: (071) 935 3463
Founded: 1989
Contact: Ms Hilary Maxfield, Director
No other locations
No public library facilities
Workplace publications
Charge for some services/products

ASH workplace services is the professional advisory service set up by ASH to help employers to take action on smoking in the workplace. It can provide sensible, practical help on establishing a smoking policy at work. The ASH workplace services smoking policy manual gives detailed instructions on how to introduce and implement a smoking policy. It allows employers to adapt the recommended policy to suit the specific needs of their own organisation. Training seminars and management consultancy services also offered.

Association for Nonsmokers' Rights (ANSR)
Melgund Centre
Melgund Terrace
Edinburgh
EH7 7BU
Tel: (031) 557 3139
Fax: –
Founded: 1981
Contact: Ms Margaret Whidden, Secretary
5 other locations
No public library facilities
Workplace publications
Charge for some services/products

Provides workplace information on the legal and medical ramifications of passive smoking. Can also offer on-the-spot workplace consultations and a sympathetic ear, with advice for passive smokers.

Cleanair – Campaign for a Smoke Free Environment (CLEANAIR)
33 Stillness Road
London SE23 1NG
Tel: (081) 690 4649
Fax: –
Founded: 1972
Contact: Mr Biman Mullick, Honorary Director
No other locations
Public library facilities
Workplace publications
Charge for some services/products

Can help individuals and organisations who wish to formulate and implement a clean air code. Provides consultation, makes recommendations and advises on workplace smoking policies. Has devised a scheme through which organisations can get their own tailor-made posters at very low cost.

Group Against Smoking in Public (GASP)
93 Cromwell Road
Bristol BS6 5EX
Tel: –
Fax: –
Founded: 1981
Contact: Ms Cecilia Farren, Founder
No other locations
No public library facilities
Workplace publications
Charge for some services/products

Provides leaflets arguing for smoke-free areas, and posters, signs and displays for use with workplace smoking policies. Can supply publications to anywhere in the country but no individual help can be given.

Quit
102 Gloucester Place
London W1H 3DA
Tel: (071) 487 2858
Fax: (071) 935 2650
Founded: 1926
Contact: Ms Nicola Chinn, Corporate Health Manager
No other locations
No public library facilities
Workplace publications
Charge for some services/products

Quit offers a range of services for employers wanting to help their staff stop smoking. Stop smoking courses, presentations and displays are run by a specially trained team of Quit co-ordinators around the country. Quit also runs the Smokers Quitline, ((071) 487 3000; 9.30–5.30, Monday–Friday; taped message rest of time), a national helpline offering telephone counselling and advice, quitpacks and referral to local stop smoking services.

Smokestop
Department of Psychology
University of Southampton
Southampton SO9 5NH
Tel: (0703) 583741
Fax: (0703) 593939
Founded: 1982
Contact: Ms Liz Batten, Director
No other locations
Public library facilities
Workplace publications

Charge for some services/products

Offers a smoking policy consultancy and seminars for managers on policy implementation. Gives presentations to smokers on how to survive the new policy and training for staff in stop-smoking groupwork and counselling. Information and advice via the HEA's smoking policies database.

Other organisations
British Heart Foundation: **69**; The British Hypnotherapy Association: **76**; Coronary Prevention Group: **69**; Dr Jan de Winter Cancer Prevention Foundation: **36**; London Black Women Health Action Project: **60**; Marie Curie Cancer Care: **38**; The National College of Hypnosis and Psychotherapy: **43**; National Council of Psychotherapists and Hypnotherapy Register: **44**; National Society for Clean Air and Environmental Protection: **57**; Regional Oncology Support Service: **38**; Sickle Cell and Thalassaemia Information Centre: **60**; Tenovus Cancer Information Centre: **39**.

The Association for Stammerers

St Margaret's House
21 Old Ford Road
London E2 9PL
Tel: (081) 983 1003
Fax: (081) 983 1553
Founded: 1978
Contact: Mr Peter Cartwright,
Director
No other locations
No public library facilities
No workplace publications
Charge for some services/products

Gives free advice and information on all aspects of stammering and stuttering, especially putting people in touch with specialist speech therapy and with self-help groups. Postal library service for members only, as well as a telephone-link and pen pal scheme; quarterly magazine and meetings throughout the UK.

Courses on social skills in the workplace planned from 1992 onwards.

Helen Arkell Dyslexia Centre (HADC)

Frensham
Farnham
Surrey GU10 3BW
Tel: (0251) 252400/4446
Fax: –
Founded: 1971
Contact: Mrs Gail Goedkoop,
Director
1 other location
Public library facilities
Workplace publications
Charge for some services/products

Leaflets available to raise awareness and understanding of dyslexia. Consultants can advise employers on screening systems to identify those in need of help with literacy skills. Products and services also available to individuals.

Other organisations

The British Hypnotherapy Association: 76; International Audiology Society: 67; Multiple Births Foundation: 103; The National Association of Laryngectomee Clubs: 38; The National College of Hypnosis and Psychotherapy: 43; National Council of Psychotherapists and Hypnotherapy Register: 44; The Psychotherapy Centre: 44; Twins and Multiple Births Association: 104.

STRESS MANAGEMENT/RELAXATION

British Association for Autogenic Training and Therapy (BAFATT)
101 Harley Street
London W1N 1DF
Tel: (071) 935 1811
Fax: (071) 935 3858
Founded: 1984
Contact: Dr Malcolm Carruthers, Chairman
100 other locations
Public library facilities
No workplace publications
Charge for some services/products

Provides training courses in autogenic training, which will bring about profound relaxation and stress release. A list of registered trainers in the UK is available on request.

International Stress Management Association (ISMA) (UK)
25 Sutherland Avenue
Leeds LS8 1BY
Tel: –
Fax: –
Founded: 1986
Contact: Mr David Bray, Information Officer
No other locations
Public library facilities
No workplace publications
Charge for some services/products

A professional body enabling people with disparate interests to meet, share experience and build on the knowledge gained. It aims to influence the thinking on stress and stress management in government, industry, commerce, professional insitutions and the public sector. The association does not provide therapy, although many of its members are therapists. It accepts that there are many approaches to dealing with stress. Written enquiries only please.

Relaxation for Living
160–170 Oatlands Drive
Weybridge
Surrey KT13 9ET
Tel: –
Fax: –
Founded: 1972
Contact: Mrs Amber Lloyd, Honorary Secretary
40 other locations
No public library facilities
Workplace publications
Charge for some services/products

Stress management through the learning and practice of physical relaxation. Small group classes are run nationwide as well as correspondence courses. In-house courses available for industry. Teacher training courses held regularly.

Other organisations
Action on Phobias: **85**; Bath Alcohol Advisory Centre: **24**; British Association for Counselling: **42**; The British Hypnotherapy Association: **76**; British Red Cross: **62**; Cancer Aftercare and Rehabilitation Society: **36**; Coronary Prevention Group: **69**; Dr Jan de Winter Cancer Prevention Foundation: **36**; Family Heart Association: **69**; Helen Arkell Dyslexia Centre: **93**; The Herpes Association: **90**; London Central Young Men's Christian Association: **86**; ME Action Campaign: **74**;

National Association for Mental Health: **77**; The National College of Hypnosis and Psychotherapy: **43**; National Council of Psychotherapists and Hypnotherapy Register: **44**; Noise Abatement Society: **57**; Phobic Action: **85**; The Psychotherapy Centre: **44**; Repetitive Strain Injury Association: **108**; Sickle Cell and Thalassaemia Information Centre: **60**; Turning Point: **55**; Women's Health Concern Ltd: **99**.

STROKE

Stroke Association
CHSA House
Whitecross Street
London EC1Y 8JJ
Tel: (071) 490 7999
Fax: (071) 490 2686
Founded: 1899
Contact: Mr IW Pratt, Secretary
10 other locations
No public library facilities
Workplace publications
Charge for some services/products

Formerly the Chest, Heart and Stroke Association, the Stroke Association offers advice and support to stroke sufferers and their families through regional stroke centres, and rehabilitation through stroke clubs, volunteer stroke schemes and stroke family support schemes. Has a small welfare fund.

Other organisations
Disabled Living Foundation: 50; The National College of Hypnosis and Psychotherapy: 43.

Cystitis and Candida

75 Mortimer Road
London N1 5AR
Tel: (071) 249 8664
Fax: –
Founded: 1966
Contact: Mrs Angela Kilmartin
No other locations
No public library facilities
No workplace publications
Charge for some services/products

Educates patients and professionals in the prevention and management of cystitis and candida through publications, lectures and personal counselling in London. Queries dealt with by telephone or letter only. Visits by appointment only.

Women's Health

52 Featherstone Street
London EC1Y 8RT
Tel: (071) 251 6580
Fax: (071) 608 0928
Founded: 1982
Contact: Women's Health
No other locations
Public library facilities
Workplace publications
Charge for some services/products

Provides information on a wide range of women's health issues and problems. In addition to leaflets and a resource library, the centre has self-help groups, runs health courses and produces a regular newsletter. The telephone helpline number above is open from 11am-5pm on Monday, Wednesday, Thursday and Friday. Letters also welcome.

Women's Health Information and Support Centre (WHISC)

Junction 7
Hazlewood Road
Northampton NN1 1LG
Tel: (0604) 39723
Fax: –
Founded: 1984
Contact: Ms Pat Quedley,
Co-ordinator
No other locations
No public library facilities
No workplace publications
No charge for services/products

Provides information on equal opportunities in health care, and women's health issues. Carries a wide range of health and health related information and can support research on request. Offers pregnancy testing and confidential counselling, group and individual support. Visitors and new volunteers welcome.

Other organisations

The British Hypnotherapy Association: **76**; Brook Advisory Centres: **40**; City Centre Project Ltd: **107**; Dr Jan de Winter Cancer Prevention Foundation: **36**; European Foundation for the Improvement of Living and Working Conditions: **107**; Family Planning Association: **40**; The Herpes Association: **90**; Just Ask Advisory and Counselling Service: **43**; Marie Stopes International: **40**; National Council of Psychotherapists and Hypnotherapy Register: **44**; The Psychotherapy Association: **44**; Twins and Multiple Births Association: **104**; Women's Health Concern Ltd: **99**.

WOMEN'S HEALTH: ABORTION

British Pregnancy Advisory Service (BPAS)
Austy Manor
Wootton Wawen
Solihull
West Midlands B95 6BX
Tel: (0564) 793225
Fax: (0564) 794935
Founded: 1968
*Contact: Ms Tara Kaufmann, Press
and Public Relations Manager*
27 other locations
No public library facilities
Workplace publications
Charge for some services/products

Offers a range of fertility-related services including pregnancy testing, abortion advice and help, contraception including emergency contraception and sterilisation. Information, counselling and educational services available at low or no cost.

Post-Abortion Counselling Service (PACS)
340 Westbourne Park Road
London W11 1EQ
Tel: (071) 221 9631
Fax: –
Founded: 1987
*Contact: Ms Pat Garrard,
Counsellor/Treasurer*
No other locations
No public library facilities
Workplace publications
Charge for some services/products

Helps women who have had abortions to explore their feelings and assists them to take responsibility for their decision. Also deals with associated issues during counselling where appropriate and offers a maximum of ten sessions before referring on for specific help if deemed necessary.

Pregnancy Advisory Service
11-13 Charlotte Street
London W1P 1HD
Tel: (071) 637 8962
Fax: (071) 323 4215
Founded: 1968
Contact: Pregnancy Advisory Service
1 other location
No public library facilities
Workplace publications
Charge for some services/products

Offers a confidential and high quality service for abortion advice and help, pregnancy testing, cervical smears, donor insemination, sterilisation and emergency contraception. Telephone the above number between 8.30am-6pm Monday to Friday, and Saturday mornings.

Other organisations
Brook Advisory Centres: **40**; Family Planning Association: **40**; Just Ask Advisory and Counselling Service: **43**; Life: **102**; London Black Women Health Action Project: **60**; Marie Stopes International: **40**; The Medical Education Trust: **41**; National Association of Natural Family Planning Teachers: **41**; National Council for One Parent Families: **104**; The Psychotherapy Centre: **44**; Women's Health: **97**.

WOMEN'S HEALTH: BREAST CARE

Breast Care and Mastectomy Association (BCMA)

15-19 Britten Street
London SW3 3TZ
Tel: (071) 867 8275
Fax: (071) 867 9303
Founded: 1973
Contact: Ms Andrea Whalley, Director
1 other location
No public library facilities
Workplace publications
Charge for some services/products

Offers emotional support and practical information to those who have or fear they may have breast cancer, or other breast problems. Helpline on (071) 867 1103. Prosthesis fitting service.

Other organisations

British Pregnancy Advisory Service: **98**; Brook Advisory Centres: **40**; Cancerlink: **35**; Cancer Aftercare and Rehabilitation Society: **36**; Cancer Relief Macmillan Fund: **36**; Dr Jan de Winter Cancer Prevention Foundation: **36**; Family Planning Association: **40**; La Leche League (Great Britain): **102**; London Black Women Health Action Project: **60**; Marie Curie Cancer Care: **38**; Marie Stopes International: **40**; Pregnancy Advisory Service: **98**; Regional Oncology Support Service: **38**; Tenovus Cancer Information Centre: **39**; Women's Health: **97**; Women's Health Concern Ltd: **99**; Women's Nationwide Cancer Control Campaign: **39**.

WOMEN'S HEALTH: HORMONE REPLACEMENT THERAPY

Women's Health Concern Ltd (WHC)

83 Earls Court Road
London W8 6EF
Tel: (071) 938 3932
Fax: (071) 376 0879
Founded: 1972
Contact: Ms Jean Jenkins, Founder President
1 other location
No public library facilities
Workplace publications
No charge for services/products

Promotes hormone replacement therapy and helps women get appropriate treatment for gynaecological conditions. Also gives specialist advice and sympathetic counselling. WHC publishes books and booklets and provides study days for doctors and nurses, and encourages scientific research.

Other organisations

Association for Post Natal Illness: **101**; Cystitis and Candida: **97**; Dr Jan de Winter Cancer Prevention Foundation: **36**; London Black Women Health Action Project: **60**; Marie Stopes International: **40**; National Association of Natural Family Planning Teachers: **41**; National Osteoporosis Society: **83**; Women's Health: **97**.

WOMEN'S HEALTH: HYSTERECTOMY

There are no organisations listed in this directory which deal specifically with hysterectomy as their main area of work. However, the following organisations can provide help and/or information in this field. For full details please refer to their entry on the page indicated opposite.

Cancerlink: **35**; Cancer Aftercare and Rehabilitation Society: **36**; Cancer Relief Macmillan Fund: **36**; Cystitis and Candida: **97**; London Black Women Health Action Project: **60**; National Osteoporosis Society: **83**; Women's Health: **97**; Women's Health Concern Ltd: **99**.

WOMEN'S HEALTH: MENOPAUSE

There are no organisations listed in this directory which deal specifically with the menopause as their main area of work. However, the following organisations can provide help and/or information in this field. For full details please refer to their entry on the page indicated opposite.

The British Hypnotherapy Association: **76**; Cystitis and Candida: **97**; Dr Jan de Winter Cancer Prevention Foundation: **36**; Family Heart Association: **69**; London Black Women Health Action Project: **60**; Marie Stopes International: **40**; National Association of Natural Family Planning Teachers: **41**; National Osteoporosis Society: **83**; Women's Health: **97**; Women's Health Concern Ltd: **99**.

WOMEN'S HEALTH: MISCARRIAGE

Miscarriage Association
c/o Clayton Hospital
Northgate
Wakefield
West Yorkshire WF1 3JS
Tel: (0924) 200799
Fax: –
Founded: 1982
Contact: Ms Kathryn Ladley, Executive Officer
160 other locations
No public library facilities
Workplace publications
Charge for some services/products

Gives advice and information on all aspects of miscarriage, early pregnancy problems and returning to work. Offers information and support for women and their families during and after miscarriage through support groups and individual contact.

Other organisations
Association for Post Natal Illness: **101**; Life: **102**; National Childbirth Trust: **103**; Post Abortion Counselling Service: **98**; The Psychotherapy Centre: **44**; Stillbirth and Neonatal Death Society: **32**; Twins and Multiple Births Association: **104**; Women's Health: **97**.

Association for Post-Natal Illness (APNI)
25 Jerdan Place
Fulham
London SW6 1BE
Tel: (071) 386 0868
Fax: –
Founded: 1979
Contact: Mrs Clare Delpech, Secretary
No other locations
No public library facilities
Workplace publications
No charge for services/products

Offers advice to depressed mothers, their families or any interested parties on a wide range of issues concerning the management and treatment of post-natal depression. Has a register of volunteers who have suffered from this illness and who support depressed mothers.

Meet-a-Mum Association (MAMA)
58 Malden Avenue
South Norwood
London SE25 4HS
Tel: (081) 656 7318
Fax: –
Founded: 1979
Contact: Mrs BJ Hallam, National Organiser
59 other locations
No public library facilities
Workplace publications
Charge for services/products

Aims to help all mothers of small children combat feelings of loneliness and isolation by putting them in touch with other mothers living nearby and by encouraging the formation of local support groups. Mothers with post-natal depression are wherever possible put in touch with another mother who has recovered.

Other organisations
La Leche League (Great Britain): 102; London Black Women Health Action Project: 60; Manic Depression Fellowship: 76; National Association for Premenstrual Syndrome: 105; National Childbirth Trust: 103; The National College of Hypnosis and Psychotherapy: 43; National Council of Psychotherapists and Hypnotherapy Register: 44; National Society for Research into Allergy: 26; Twins and Multiple Births Association: 104; Women's Health: 97; Women's Health Concern Ltd: 99.

WOMEN'S HEALTH: PREGNANCY AND WORKING PARENTS

Cry-Sis Helpline

BM Cry-Sis
London WC1N 3XX
Tel: (071) 404 5011
Fax: –
Founded: 1981
Contact: Ms Janice Bradbury,
National Training Officer
150 other locations
No public library facilities
Workplace publications
Charge for some services/products

Can give support, sympathy and tips to parents.

Exploring Parenthood

Latimer Education Centre
194 Freston Road
London W10 6TT
Tel: (081) 960 1678
Fax: (081) 964 1827
Founded: 1982
Contact: Exploring Parenthood
2 other locations
No public library facilities
Workplace publications
Charge for some services/products

Offers the New Parents Project advisory service for parents and employers to help them cope with the stresses and strains of becoming parents while remaining in employment. Runs a counselling and advice service for parents on all aspects of parenting with professional counselling available.

La Leche League (LLL) (Great Britain)

BM 3424
London WC1N 3XX
Tel: (071) 242 1278
Fax: –
Founded: 1980
Contact: Ms Esther Culpin,
Director/professional liaison/public
relations
No other locations
Public library facilities
Workplace publications
Charge for some services/products

Can assist employers and employees to promote working conditions appropriate for nursing mothers and can enhance the expertise of health professionals involved in obstetric and child-care policy making.

Provides regular support meetings, a range of breastfeeding publications, telephone counselling and a professionally backed service for special breastfeeding queries.

Can provide information on other health areas in relation to breast-feeding.

Life

Life House
1a Newbold Terrace
Leamington Spa
Warwickshire CV32 4EA
Tel: (0926) 421587
Fax: (0926) 336497
Founded: 1970
Contact: Mrs Anne Dibb, Hon.
National Caring Officer
200 other locations
No public library facilities

Workplace publications
Charge for some services/products

Offers help and support to unsupported pregnant women and families through free pregnancy testing, pregnancy and abortion counselling and temporary accommodation (women only – pregnant or with babies), although it should be noted that the accommodation service is not free of charge. Free post-abortion counselling is also available. For the national hotline please call (0926) 311511.

Maternity Alliance
15 Britannia Street
London WC1X 9JP
Tel: (071) 837 1265
Fax: (071) 837 1273
Founded: 1980
Contact: Ms Mary Shackle,
Information Officer
No other locations
No public library facilities
Workplace publications
Charge for some services/products

Runs a telephone information service on all aspects of pregnancy and new parenthood. Leaflets on pregnancy rights at work, benefits available and preconception care are free to individuals and £0.10 each to organisations.

Multiple Births Foundation (MBF)
Queen Charlotte's and Chelsea Hospital
Goldhawk Road
London W6 0XG
Tel: (081) 748 4666 x 5201
Fax: (081) 748 4666 x 5281
Founded: 1988
Contact: Ms Barbara Read,
Secretary/Administrator

2 other locations
No public library facilities
Workplace publications
Charge for some services/products

Gives advice and support to families with twins (or more) through twins clinics, letters and telephone calls; to professionals; research workers and the media.

National Childbirth Trust (NCT)
Alexandra House
Oldham Terrace
London W3 6NH
Tel: (081) 992 8637
Fax: (081) 992 5929
Founded: 1957
Contact: Ms Shirleyanne Seel, Acting
Head: Policy and Development
374 other locations
Public library facilities
Workplace publications
Charge for some services/products

Offers information and support in pregnancy, childbirth and early parenthood and aims to enable every parent to make informed choices. It can help with running ante-natal classes for employers and generally advise on maternity issues and breastfeeding for working mothers.

Many local branches offer a working mothers' support group plus other specialist support services.

National Council for One Parent Families
255 Kentish Town Road
London NW5 2LX
Tel: (071) 267 1361
Fax: (071) 482 4851
Founded: 1918
Contact: Ms Sui-Wan Goody,
Librarian
No other locations
Public library facilities
Workplace publications
Charge for some services/products

A unique library is available to provide resources on all topics associated with lone parenthood, with briefings and reports produced on a regular basis providing up-to-date information on current policy developments.

Free information packs and booklets are available and there are regional Return to Work courses which address issues such as childcare, finances, confidence building and employment and training opportunities.

Lone parent self-help groups can subscribe, at a reduced rate, to the information manual and associated services.

New Ways to Work
309 Upper Street
London N1 2TY
Tel: (071) 226 4026
Fax: (071) 354 2978
Founded: 1980
Contact: Mr Charles Monkcom, Joint
Co-ordinator
No other locations
No public library facilities
Workplace publications
Charge for some services/products

Can help employers to formulate a flexible work arrangement policy and provides a free telephone and enquiry service to anyone who wishes to learn about flexible work arrangements: job sharing, part-time work, term-time working, employment breaks, annual hours agreements and working from home.

Twins and Multiple Births Association
(TAMBA)
PO Box 30
Little Sutton
South Wirral L66 1TH
Tel: (051) 348 0020
Fax: as tel.
Founded: 1978
Contact: Gina Siddons, Administrator
No other locations
No public library facilities
Workplace publications
Charge for some services/products

Works to promote public and professiona awareness of the needs of families with twins, triplets or more. Has specialist support groups throughout the country to help families and give access to professional advice. Listening and information service: 6pm-11pm (weekdays) 8am-11pm (weekends). A telephone helpline will be available shortly.

Working for Childcare
77 Holloway Road
London N7 8JZ
Tel: (071) 700 0281
Fax: (071) 700 1105
Founded: 1984
Contact: Information Officer
No other locations
No public library facilities
Workplace publications
Charge for some services/products

Undertakes research into employment related childcare issues and offers consultancy services to employers on childcare policy and development. Assistance is given to employers in setting up nurseries or in running other schemes such as childcare vouchers. Can also help with management consultancy for existing childcare provisions.

Working Mothers Association (WMA)
77 Holloway Road
London N7 8JZ
Tel: (071) 700 5771
Fax: (071) 700 1105
Founded: 1985
Contact: Ms Irene Pilia, Information Officer
No other locations
No public library facilities
Workplace publications
Charge for some services/products

A self-help organisation for working parents and their children. Through a network of local groups, it provides an informal support system for working mothers. On a national level it offers information and advice to interested organisations, policy-makers and employers.

Other organisations
Action and Research for Multiple Sclerosis: **80**; British Diabetic Association: **48**; The British Hypnotherapy Association: **76**; City Centre Project Ltd: **107**; The Herpes Association: **90**; London Hazards Centre: **107**; Marie Stopes International: **40**; The Medical Education Trust: **41**; The National College of Hypnosis and Psychotherapy: **43**; Positively Women: **71**; The Psychotherapy Centre: **44**; Sickle Cell and Thalassaemia Information Centre: **60**; Women's Health: **97**.

WOMEN'S HEALTH: PREMENSTRUAL SYNDROME

National Association for Premenstrual Syndrome (NAPS)
PO Box 72
Sevenoaks
Kent TN13 1QX
Tel: (0732) 459378
Fax: –
Founded: 1984
Contact: Mrs Althea Wheeler, Office Manager
No other locations
No public library facilities
Workplace publications
Charge for some services/products

Can advise employers of the problems which result from pre-menstrual syndrome and post-natal depression in relation to efficiency, attendance and relations with co-workers. Can advise the individual on how to control PMS and PND through diet or diet plus hormone treatment as well as giving information on how to cope with the problems of shift work.

NAPS can supply speakers to inform employers and employees about the problems and ways in which the illnesses can be dealt with; and can liaise with occupational health staff.

Premenstrual Society (PREMSOC)
PO Box 429
Addlestone
Surrey KT15 1DZ
Tel: (0932) 872560
Fax: –
Founded: 1986
Contact: Mr Michael Brush,
Co-Chairman and Adviser
No other locations
No public library facilities
Workplace publications
Charge for some services/products

Believes that both employers and employees should be fully aware of the loss of working efficiency and the personal distress caused by premenstrual syndrome and that women can be helped if adequate information and support is available. Enquiries relating to premenstrual syndrome are welcome at all times either from organisations or individuals preferably by letter, but telephone queries accepted from professionals.

Other organisations
Association for Post Natal Illness: 101; The British Hypnotherapy Association: **76**; Brook Advisory Centres: **40**; London Black Women Health Action Project: **60**; Marie Stopes International: **40**; The National College of Hypnosis and Psychotherapy: **43**; National Council of Psychotherapists and Hypnotherapy Register: **44**; National Society for Research into Allergy: **26**; The Psychotherapy Centre: **44**; Women's Health: **97**; Women's Health Concern Ltd: **99**.

City Centre Project Ltd

32-35 Featherstone Street
London EC1Y 8QX
Tel: (071) 608 1338
Fax: –
Founded: 1984
*Contact: Ms Gill Kirton, Health and
Safety Officer*
No other locations
Public library facilities
Workplace publications
Charge for some services/products

Consultancy service offered with
workplace visits followed up by a
written report containing advice on
improving the office environment.
Can give follow up health and safety
training for management and workers.

Free information and advice offered
to individuals or groups of office
workers with counselling and support
available where necessary.

European Foundation for the Improvement of Living and Working Conditions (EFILWIC)

Loughlinstown House
Shankill
County Dublin
Ireland
Tel: (010) 3531 2826888
Fax: (010) 3531 2826456
Founded: 1975
*Contact: Mr Robert Anderson,
Research Manager*
No other locations
Public library facilities
Workplace publications
No charge for services/products

Reviews legislation, policy development and practice related to workplace
health promotion in EC member
states, for example, *Innovative workplace action for health: an overview of
the situation in seven EC countries.*
Library facilities are by arrangement.

Health and Safety Advice Centre (HASAC)

Unit 304
The Argent Centre
60 Frederick Street
Birmingham B1 3HS
Tel: (021) 236 0801
Fax: (021) 236 7842
Founded: 1980
*Contact: Mr Terry McGuire, Health
and Safety Adviser*
6 other locations
Public library facilities
Workplace publications
No charge for services/products

Provides information, services and
resources on hazards at work and in
the community for those in greatest
need and/or with least access to them:
individual workers, trade unions, resi-
dents, tenants and community groups
and small businesses which lack spe-
cialised health and safety staff.

Hazards dealt with: physical agents,
substances, processes, industrial accidents and health, compensation for
industrial injury, noise induced hearing loss, labour law, trade unions.

London Hazards Centre

Headland House
308 Grays Inn Road
London WC1X 8DS
Tel: (071) 837 5605
Fax: -
Founded: 1984

Contact: Ms Maggie Alexander,
Publications Co-ordinator
No other locations
Public library facilities
Workplace publications
Charge for some services/products

Primarily a free advice service for workplace and community groups in London but will answer queries nationally. Can help organised workplace groups (principally those in trades unions) to develop policies specific to health and safety matters, and aid in their implementation.

A helpline is open from 2pm–5pm weekdays and library visits are by appointment only.

Problems are dealt with by providing advice, information, publications, information research/online searches, reports inspections and speakers.

Other organisations
Association for Nonsmokers' Rights: **91**; National Back Pain Association: **30**; New Ways to Work: **104**; Relaxation for Living: **94**; Royal Society for the Prevention of Accidents: **19**.

WORKPLACE HEALTH AND SAFETY: REPETITIVE STRAIN INJURIES

Repetitive Strain Injury (RSI) Association
Christ Church
Redford Way
Uxbridge
Middlesex UB8 1SZ
Tel: (0895) 431134
Founded: 1988
Contact: Mr R Mulelly, Chairman
No other locations
No public library facilities
Workplace publications
Charge for some services/products

Can help formulate policies dealing with the management of RSI in the workplace, as well as promoting self-help groups. Offers an advice and information service to RSI sufferers and other interested parties.

Other organisations
City Centre Project: **107**; Health and Safety Advice Centre: **107**; London Hazards Centre: **107**; The Medico 9 Organisation: **62**; National Back Pain Association: **30**; National Society for Research into Allergy: **26**; Royal Society for the Prevention of Accidents: **19**; Society for the Prevention of Asbestosis and Industrial Diseases: **29**; Women's Health Information and Support Centre: **97**.

WORKPLACE HEALTH AND SAFETY: VDU-RELATED

There are no organisations listed in this directory which deal specifically with VDU-related problems as their main area of work. However, the following organisations can provide help and/or information in this field. For full details please refer to their entry on the page indicated below.

Association of Optometrists: **33**; City Centre Project Ltd: **107**; Health and Safety Advice Centre: **107**; London Hazards Centre: **107**; Miscarriage Association: **100**; National Back Pain Association: **30**; Repetitive Strain Injury Association: **108**; Royal Society for the Prevention of Accidents: **19**; Society for the Prevention of Asbestosis and Industrial Diseases: **29**.

Appendix I: Alphabetical index by subject area

Appendix 2: Alphabetical index by organisation name